DOUBT,
TIME,
VIOLENCE

DOUBT TIME VIOLENCE

Piotr
Hoffman

DOUBT,
TIME,
VIOLENCE

The
University
of Chicago
Press

Piotr Hoffman is associate professor of philosophy at the University of Nevada, Reno, and the author of *The Anatomy of Idealism: Passivity and Activity in Kant, Hegel, and Marx* and *The Human Self and the Life and Death Struggle*

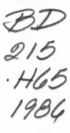

The University of Chicago Press, Chicago 60637
The University of Chicago Press, Ltd., London
© 1986 by The University of Chicago
All rights reserved. Published 1986

Printed in the United States of America
95 94 93 92 91 90 89 88 87 86 5 4 3 2 1

LIBRARY OF CONGRESS CATALOGING-IN-PUBLICATION DATA

Hoffman, Piotr.
  Doubt, time, violence.

  Bibliography: p.
  Includes index.
  1. Belief and doubt.   2. Time.   3. Violence.
I. Title.
BD215.H65   1986   121'.5   86-16127
ISBN 0-226-34791-5

Contents

Abbreviations

Works frequently cited in the text and Notes have been abbreviated. Full bibliographic information is available in the reference Bibliography of Works Cited which follows Notes at the end of the book.

HR, I–II   R. Descartes, *The Philosophical Works of Descartes*

Enc. II   G. W. F. Hegel, *Hegel's Philosophy of Nature: Part Two of the Encyclopaedia of the Philosophical Sciences*

Enc. III   G. W. F. Hegel, *Hegel's Philosophy of Mind: Part Three of the Encyclopaedia of the Philosophical Sciences*

SL   G. W. F. Hegel, *Hegel's Science of Logic*

PhM   G. W. F. Hegel, *The Phenomenology of Mind*

BPP   M. Heidegger, *The Basic Problems of Phenomenology*

BT   M. Heidegger, *Being and Time*

ILH   A. Kojève, *Introduction à la lecture de Hegel*

Introduction

With Descartes's *ego cogito,* philosophy took a new direction, and it was thus set on a collision course with the ordinary, commonsensical attitudes and beliefs of the everyday life. In effect, if the beginning of philosophical inquiry is identified with an act of methodical doubt through which the thinking self suspends its assent to the evidences of everyday life, then such a mode of philosophizing will depart inevitably from the commonsensical standards of intelligibility and truth. Can we discover a link between the ordinary and the philosophical points of view while doing justice to the claims of both of them? I think we can, and I intend to show this by arguing the two following points: (1) some of the mainstream problems of modern philosophy stem from a focus on violence, and (2) an analysis of violence allows one to discover the continuity between the philosophical and the ordinary points of view.

Whereas the importance of violence for modern political philosophy—from Hobbes and Machiavelli to Hegel and Marx—is generally recognized, this recognition does not extend to other areas of philosophical inquiry. Yet, a conception and an experience of violence are just beneath the surface of the specifically modern idea of human self. While the full justification of this claim will have to await the Conclusion of the present study, we can give the reader a general sense of where we are going by bringing out some close parallels between Descartes and Hobbes. These two philosophers are, in effect, the founding fathers of modern epistemology and political theory. The importance of their systems for the subsequent developments of modernity cannot be overestimated.

In general, the modern era in philosophy begins with and is built around the idea of an autonomous self set over against the world and engaged in an active search of its identity. The true and the good are not to be found—as they were in the Renaissance and throughout the Middle Ages—in a meaningful order of cosmos. The self collects itself from the world and turns inward. It is only from such an isolated, individual subject that the justification of the human knowledge or of the moral and political obligation can proceed. The self is the Archimedean point, the ultimate ground of any such justification and reconstruction of knowledge and reality. For that reason, the self must first emerge as freed from its naive, uncritical ties to its surroundings. No external authority ought to impose its *diktat* upon the deliberations of the self. In the Cartesian quest for certainty, in Hobbes's point of departure in the "state of nature," the human individual stands alone, thrown back upon himself and his own experiences and thoughts.

With this general picture in mind, let us focus upon the more specific issue of the role of violence in both Descartes and Hobbes.

Let us note, to begin with, that the cogito of Descartes emerges from the very beginning as a center of subjective *activity*. It is misleading to read Descartes as being interested in simply drawing a line between material bodies on the one hand and our mental life on the other hand. To be more precise, the distinction between the mental and the material is derived from and based upon the distinction between thinking and everything that is not a mode of thought. It is true, of course, that such mental faculties as, for example, perception and imagination are considered by Descartes as belonging to the cogito. But they belong to the cogito only insofar as they are modes of thought (HR, I, 157), that is, only insofar as they include implicit *judgments*. Descartes explains this clearly in a passage from the *Principles of Philosophy:* "To take an example, if I persuade myself that there is an earth because I touch or see it, by that very same fact, and by a yet stronger reason, I should be persuaded that my thought exists; because it may be that I *think* I touch the earth even though there is possibly no earth existing at all, but it is not possible that I who form this *judgment* and my mind which *judges* thus, should be non-existent; *and so in other cases*" (HR, I, 223; my italics). Descartes clearly means this conclusion to be of universal scope, and it is the same conclusion he arrives at while deploying his main argument in the *Second Meditation*. After he has analyzed his knowledge of the piece of wax and shown us that a material object's identity cannot be grasped by senses or imagination but by intellect alone, he turns to a different and still more troubling issue: What if that entire piece of wax that he thought he identified through a careful exercise of his intellect were to have been not a genuine material object but an illusion to begin with? The question is perfectly justified, since Descartes is considering that famous wax example *after* he has offered sufficient support to his methodical skepticism. We are now at a stage of the argument where we must consider ourselves as deprived of any grounds for our belief in the reality of material bodies—and hence also in the reality of that piece of wax. But, at the same time, our doubt about the reality of what we see implies the certainty of our thought of seeing: it may be the case that there is no wax that I can see, but it remains the case that *I think I see* (HR, I, 156) that piece of wax. And the expression "I think I see" does not refer, in general, to my having a "representation" or an "idea" of wax but, quite specifically, to my *judging* that I see the real wax (ibid.). Even while I doubt the correctness of my judgment, I cannot doubt that I judge, that I exist as judging, and that I exercise my judgment about this particular perception of wax. The perception belongs to the cogito—to the realm of what is absolutely certain to me—insofar as it is an element of my judgment.

Descartes's analysis of our knowledge of the piece of wax, as well as his entire treatment of the cogito in the *Second Meditation,* fits into a broader project that he had been pursuing ever since the *Rules for the Direction of the Mind.* If the cogito is essentially an intellectual activity of judging, and if in judgments the intellect's concepts are brought to bear upon our perceptions or thoughts, then judgments are the devices with the aid of which our intellect forms its own representation of reality. These moves, anticipating the positions of Kant—the moves through which Descartes brings out the active role of human intellect in shaping knowledge and the picture of the world as it is accessible to knowledge—are an inherent part of Descartes's strategy.[1] In effect, the self's activity of judging is governed by certain concepts which, on account of their *necessity,* cannot be derived from experience but from intellect alone. While Descartes's favorite examples are borrowed—in the

Rules as well as in the *Fifth Meditation*—from arithmetic and geometry, he also makes it clear that these two sciences are but the privileged "illustrations" (HR, I, 13) of a more "general science" (ibid.) which is the science of "order and measurement" (ibid.) as such. These two concepts, Descartes believes, are the most general conditions of the possibility of our intellect's cognitive activity. Hence the science of order and measurement will bring out "the rudiments of human reason" (HR, I, II). Descartes's later terminology of "innate" ideas ought not to obscure what has always been the real issue for him: the concepts of order and measurement are not some mental items making up the furniture of the mind but, first and foremost, the necessary rules that underlie the mind's ability to know anything. In effect (HR, I, 55–65), any act of knowledge must succeed in establishing a "comparison" between the contents to be known. According to Descartes, such a comparison cannot be established unless those contents are made uniform by their subsumption under the scale of order and measurement. Furthermore, since the concepts of order and measurement are drawn from intellect itself, and since no knowledge of material world is possible without those concepts, anything we claim to know about the world will have to be considered as standing in a relation to human intellect and its concepts.[2] In this respect, the examples given in the *Rules*—Descartes analyzes how we can know a body (HR, I, 41), a magnet (HR, I, 47), a sensory quality (HR, I, 56)— are in full conformity with the later doctrine as exemplified in the famous account of our capacity to know and to identify that changing piece of wax.[3]

But this also means that the Cartesian *ratio* emerges as a tool of human power. Our representation of reality is not a passive given but a product of an intellectual construction. Moreover, this active function of human intelligence is the harbinger of the forthcoming *practical* elevation of man to the status of the effective "master of nature." This crucial motive of modernity is implicitly contained in Descartes's picture of human knowledge. By subsuming nature under his own conceptual framework, man brings the former within his cognitive grip—a step soon to be followed by his sustained drive to establish his dominion over the natural environment with the forces of science and technology.[4]

The move through which the Cartesian self collects itself from the world and turns inward is the act of methodical doubt. Due to this doubt, the self ceases to *take for granted* the ways of the every-day world and asserts itself as capable of a truly autonomous thought. Now doubt, in Descartes, is imposed upon the self by the hypothesis of the *evil demon*. This thesis will be argued in detail in Chapter 1, but we can point out from the very beginning that this is how Descartes himself presents the emergence of the cogito in his most important philosophical work. When plunged in the attitude of universal doubt by the prospect of being at the mercy of the evil demon, Descartes comes to learn both that he exists (HR, I, 150) and that he is a thinking being (HR, I, 151). Thus, what throws Descartes back upon the certainty of his own thought—and of it alone—is the view of himself as being under a *threat*. As we shall see in Chapter 1, Descartes goes to great pains to point out the evil demon's *power*. For in order to be compelled to adopt the stance of doubt when confronted with the threat of the evil demon, I must abandon all my hope of controlling or manipulating that demon; and I will not abandon such a hope unless I see the demon as a power beyond the reach of all my powers. In the last analysis, then, it is my recognition of a threatening power which I cannot control, that will force me to suspend my naive, precritical forms of life and thought.

Descartes's account of the human self's *education by violence* comes astonishingly close to the teachings of Hobbes. For Hobbes, the only limit of a man's power is the power of another man. Now, the power of another man imposes itself upon a human individual in a violent encounter—real or envisioned as an ever-threatening pos-sibility—which turns into a genuine life-and-death struggle. This prospect of a violent struggle with the other stops my immediate impulse to extend my power and suspends the entire background of illusory, wishful thinking associated with that impulse.

A seeming confusion in Hobbes's definition of "power" will lead us to the heart of the issue. On the one hand, power is defined as man's "present means to obtain some future apparent Good."[5] The adjective "apparent" with which Hobbes qualifies his refer-ence to the "good" ought not to be seen as embroiling him in some unwarranted metaphysical distinction between appearance and real-ity. The function of the adjective is here to serve as the indication of Hobbes's typically modern view of the relation between the good and the desirable. The good is "apparent," for the goodness of this or that item can be defined only in terms of its desirability to this or that agent at this or that stage of his life history. There is no good over and above the desirable: the good and the evil are not established in the order of things but injected into the world by human appetites and aversions. As for the "means" covered by the term "power," Hobbes divides them into two classes, the natural powers and the instrumental powers, and gives several examples of both.[6] But Hobbes also puts forward a different—and seemingly unrelated—definition of power: that it "is simply no more but the excess of the power of one [man] above that of another."[7] Needless to say, from a strictly logical point of view, the definition of "power" in terms of "excess of power" must be considered most unfortunate. Yet the main thrust of Hobbes's thinking is here clear enough: the assesment of my power involves an essential comparison of that power with the power of others; power is thus a relative term which applies to me only insofar as I stand in relation to other men. Whatever means and capacities I can deploy at any given moment, they cannot be viewed as "powers" unless they give me an advantage over the means and the capacities of other human agents. A different and more important question can now be raised. What is the relationship of the two definitions of power? Why couldn't I be said to be in possession of some means to gratify my desires even if these means would not give me any advantage over the means marshaled by someone else? I desire an apple or a pear; I stretch out my hand and pick the fruit from the branch; I have thereby exercised one of my ("natural") powers without any relation to the power of another man. Clearly, then, it seems that power ascriptions can be made independently of any consideration of the agent's relation to other agents.

Hobbes, however, believes this not to be the case. After all, he would reply immediately to our example, somebody could have prevented me from picking that desirable, ripe fruit from the branch; if I succeeded in gratifying my desire it's because my action was not *hindered* by the actions of another man. This was, in effect, the very reason Hobbes gave for his second definition of power (ibid.). My "present means to obtain some future apparent Good" are *effective* means only if I can rely upon them in spite of the obstacle represented by another man. If the other is in a position of preventing me from fulfilling my desires, then all my means and capacities are not "powers" for the very simple and entirely sufficient reason that they will be of no use to me at all in bringing within my reach that future apparent good. In the end, then, power ascriptions must always reflect an individual's position with respect to other individuals.

But man, in general, cannot be satisfied with a moderate amount of power. In a famous statement, Hobbes "put[s] for a generall inclination of mankind a perpetuall and restlesse desire of Power after power, that ceaseth only in Death."[8] He at once (ibid.) gives the reason for this generalization: some men (the vain, the glory seekers, as he explains elsewhere) are simply not content with moderate power; others—those who would be satisfied with moderate power if left to themselves—must strive for more and more power since they are forced to go on building up their defenses against the never-ceasing challenges of the first kind of men. All human relations—both peaceful and violent—can be understood only against the background of that generalized and perpetual striving after power.

Hobbes lays down another important premise: the *value* of a man is simply his price, that is, whatever it is that other men would give for the use of his powers.[9] Hence it is altogether impossible to have a sense of one's own worth without depending upon the evaluations and appraisals of the others. A man whose opinion of his value would not correspond to the latter's actual price to other men would be simply deluding himself.[10] Since, as we already know, man must strive to amass an ever-greater concentration of power, and since no man can know the "true value" (ibid.) of this power without having it judged by the others, it follows that every human individual will aspire to maximize his value as measured by others. The recognition of my value by others is manifested in their multifarious ways of *honoring* me; while their lack of recognition of my value is expressed in acts of *dishonor* (ibid.). Every human individual, therefore, must strive for honor and avoid dishonor. Let us stress again that all the strivings and motivations we have mentioned so far are operative both in society and in a state of nature.[11]

My striving for the validation by others has a more *practical* side to it as well. For, first, of all the means and capacities that I may command as my powers, other *people* are the greatest powers a human agent can ever hope to have.[12] Now love and fear that people feel toward me are the sure signs of their recognition of my value,[13] and, quite naturally, those who love me and fear me will supply me with service and assistance.[14] It follows that my striving for and achievement of honors will not only validate my value but will also allow me to expand my powers by enlisting other men under my banner. Thus my overall attitude toward the other is composed of two opposite stances: the other is a blessing since he can contribute most to the increase of my powers; but he is also a curse since he is in a position to deprive me of any power whatsoever.

The cases of love and fear are the best examples with which to illustrate the novelty of Hobbes's account of *passions*. To fear or to love does not mean to be subject to some blind and inarticulate affection. It is my grasp of the other's power that will induce the passion I feel toward him; passion is thus based on my *conception* of his power in comparison to my own power and to the power of others. In Hobbes's terminology, then, the passions we feel toward a person are determined by our conception of his "value"; they are thus our ways of honoring or dishonoring him. Passions, therefore, are items in a constant power struggle among men: to succeed in inducing fear or love into the other's breast is to succeed in increasing one's power over him. This is why being loved or feared gives us pleasure. While the pleasures of the senses concern what is merely useful to us, all pleasures of the soul are due to that feeling of increasing our power over the other.[15] Crude sensory pleasures aside, pleasure too cannot be construed as an inarticulate sensation: pleasure is the sure sign of our success in the struggle for precedence and honor.

In the absence of effective political constraints such a struggle must end, inevitably, in a state of generalized violence. As Leo Strauss has shown brilliantly,[16] it is vanity[17] that allows Hobbes to explain this inevitability of violence.[18] For vanity, Hobbes thinks, is the only *unlimited* aspiration: man's striving for precedence over others knows no end, and hence the clash with the similar aspirations of other men cannot be avoided. Thus, even if some individuals were sensible enough to satisfy themselves with a moderate amount of power, they would be drawn into an unending struggle by the seekers of glory. Hobbes reproduces this argument again and again.[19] It is true that he considers "competition" and "diffidence" to be the contributing sources of human violence. But, first, men strike out of diffidence only because they suspect a *prior* hostility of other men[20]; diffidence, therefore, cannot be the ultimate cause of the struggle. And, second, it is not at all clear why competition for goods—as opposed to an unceasing "competition for power,"[21] which must itself be explained—would have to result necessarily in struggle unless we posit extreme scarcity of goods as the natural precondition of every form of human association. Hobbes does not want to make such a totally unwarranted assumption, and he is consistent enough to tell us that only vanity can necessarily lead to human struggle[22]; competition itself, he says, can cause violence only occasionally.[23]

But the unthinking, impulsive assertion of the self bent on achieving more and more power will soon find its limit in the power of the other. The life-and-death struggle which erupts or is about to erupt awakens the "fear of violent death"[24] in the heart of human agents. This fear is a passion, and, like all passions, it is shot through with the agent's conception and assessment of his own power: from "death . . . we expect . . . the loss of *all* power."[25] The life-and-death struggle, therefore, brings man face-to-face with a very real possibility of the sudden termination of all the possibilities of maximizing his power. Since man *is* bent at maximizing his power, he will have to refrain from violence in order to be able to secure any power at all. This recoiling from violence is induced by the agent's fearful conception of death as the total and irrevocable loss of power.

The self's education by violence is now completed. Man's naive identification with the unthinking impulse to assert himself—and with all the illusions and biases nourished by that impulse—is destroyed by the threatening power of the other. From now on man will think and act independently of the wishful thinking governing the life of his immediate self. He has now reached a radically new point of departure from which he will first envision and then build a new world—the world of social and political institutions.[26]

Let us conclude this brief review. Crucial to the accounts of both Descartes and Hobbes is a conception of human vulnerability and exposure to a threatening power. When brought face-to-face with such a power, man finds himself thrown back upon himself, his naive ties with the world severed, his security—both practical and cognitive—gone. It is true, of course, that while Hobbes talks explicitly about human violence—for the threat to me is simply the threat of other men—in Descartes man finds himself vulnerable to the power of the "evil demon." But what if Descartes's conception of the menacing demon were to have been a reflection of those more tangible threats that Hobbes, at the same juncture in history, has recognized as the background of human life and association? What if only on the assumption of a profoundly *human* nature of Descartes's demon could we make sense of the entire problematic that Descartes's theory of doubt generates to begin with?

The purpose of the present study is to argue that some of the mainstream problematic of modern philosophy is indeed intelligible only when placed in a context in which the phenomenon of human violence is of paramount importance. I hope to produce adequate support for this claim in the course of a close discussion of two pivotal philosophical issues which I have selected as the testing grounds for my interpretation. The two issues are those of Doubt and Time.

No *new analysis* of these two problems will—or can—be offered here. What I have aimed for is a *new solution* to the problems as they have been defined and analyzed in the writings of some of the major philosophers: in Descartes, in Hegel, and, above all, in Heidegger's *Being and Time*.[27] While it would be impossible for me to justify *beforehand* the choice of precisely these three thinkers, I do hope that the reasons for my choice will become clear to the reader as he makes his way through the book. For, in my judgment, Descartes, Hegel, and Heidegger have attacked the problems of doubt and time with as much insight and logic as was altogether possible given certain assumptions and constraints defining our recent modes of philosophizing. My main purpose in this book will be to show how the very standards and requirements set forth by those three thinkers themselves can be met only if we consider our philosophical discourse as being implicitly discourse of and about human violence. I will not, therefore, be adopting a perspective external to modern philosophy but will instead attempt to follow up on the ultimate implications of its own conceptual framework. By this route I will be arriving, in the Conclusion, at a philosophical position I have already explored and argued for elsewhere.[28] The present work, therefore, is not to be seen as a contribution to the history of ideas but as a philosophical study. The problematic discovered and analyzed by Descartes, Hegel, and Heidegger, among others, is very much a live issue in contemporary philosophical discussions. An attempt to solve some of the puzzles generated by this problematic will, I hope, contribute to philosophy itself.

I would like to express my thanks to colleagues and friends whose helpful comments contributed to shape the final version of the book. Hubert L. Dreyfus, Charles B. Guignon, and John Mc-Cumber have read the first draft of the manuscript and have suggested several changes which substantially improved the presentation of my argument. Jacques d'Hondt has found time to discuss with me Hegel and Kojève. And a conversation with Bill Blattner allowed me to gain additional clarity about Heidegger's views on time.

DOUBT

Chapter 1

Descartes's analysis of sensory illusions is often presented as a textbook case of an argument supporting the skeptical conclusions. In effect, Descartes's reasoning (HR, I, 145) seems to follow the familiar skeptical line: since the senses have misled us in the past, and since it is not prudent to trust someone who has deceived us even once, we should refrain from giving our assent to any belief stemming from the senses. The examples given by Descartes himself belong to the traditional arsenal of the skeptic. Descartes talks about straight sticks looking bent when immersed in water (HR, II, 252); he mentions the man ill with jaundice who sees everything as yellow (HR, I, 44); he notes that food has a bitter taste to a sick man (HR, I, 313), and so on.

But it is not clear at all how these and similar examples could ever lead us to the skeptical conclusions. A number of questions must first be answered, and the answers seem to be lacking so far. Do I really have the right to universalize my doubt on the grounds that in *some* cases I have been deceived by the senses? Certainly not, if I intended to arrive at the conclusion via an ordinary inductive inference from those very few cases I am familiar with. Conversely, if my claim is genuinely universal, then how can it be based on something other than the merely conceptual analysis of the notions ("perception," "illusion," etc.) involved? And then the difficulty is clear: since my (skeptical) conclusions depart so radically from the naive realism of common sense, they cannot be based on the *ordinary* understanding of the concepts of perception and illusion. But then what *are* my conclusions based on? Am I not exploring the implications of an arbitrary and fanciful mode of thinking which has no connection at all with the attitudes of the ordinary life?

There seems to be one easy way of dismissing such questions as irrelevant. One can try to recast Descartes's argument in the form of a conjunction of some empirical observations with an additional rule allowing us to generalize the doubt. Formally, such a presentation of Descartes's move can be made quite transparent. Descartes has noticed that (1) in some cases he has been unable to find a difference between a sensory illusion and a genuine perception; but (2) all cases ought to be considered as equally unreliable in this respect, for when we examine them carefully we notice that they are all equally and similarly cases of being presented with mere mental images; hence (3) in no case can we ever be sure that we are having genuine perception and not a sensory illusion.

Now, this is undoubtedly the position Descartes ultimately adopts while pursuing the line of methodical skepticism. But he neither intends to nor is he capable of arriving at this position through a mere analysis of sensory illusions. The reader who expects Descartes to justify his doubt by the argument from illusion alone will soon be disappointed: "But it may be that although the senses sometimes deceive us concerning things which are hardly perceptible, or very far away, there are yet many others to be met with as to which we cannot reasonably have any doubt, although we recognize them by their means . . . And how could I deny that these hands and this body are mine, were it not perhaps that I compare myself to certain persons, devoid of sense . . . But they are mad and I should not be any the less insane were I to follow examples so extravagant" (HR, I, 145).

At least one lesson can be learned immediately from this passage. As we just noted, if the examination of sensory illusions is to carry us toward the skeptical position, then rule (2) above must be appealed to, and then a way must be found of providing support for that crucial claim about all cases of sensory awareness being similar in their status of mere mental images. But Descartes says clearly that our sensory experiences are very different in this respect. To some of them—to most of them—it would be, he says, "extravagant" to apply the label of a mere image in one's mind. Under normal and typical circumstances we should have no doubt that our sensory cognition reaches out toward independent objects instead of being immersed in our private mental contents.

The upshot of Descartes's analysis of illusions can now be presented in a more systematic way. When I focus only upon the mere fact that in some cases I am unable to tell the difference between a veridical perception and a sensory illusion, I not only lack sufficient grounds for universalizing my doubt, but, furthermore:

(a) I have not suspended the legitimacy of the concept of veridical perception,

(b) I still take it for granted that there are (and I am familiar with) cases of veridical perception, and

(c) I label some of my perceptions illusory only through a contrast with (against the background of) a body of reliable perceptions providing me with a *norm* through which I can identify some of my perceptions as deceptive; to extend my doubt over the normal perceptions themselves would be "extravagant."

But these three components are the very same ones that govern our ordinary evaluations and assessments. A housewife inspecting a bunch of eggs does not doubt for a moment—if she thinks about it at all—that the concept of a fresh egg is legitimate; she does not doubt having smelt or tasted some items identifiable by such a concept; and she is unwilling to buy rotten eggs precisely on account of their perceivable difference with the fresh ones. Similarly, when I begin to doubt that the Christmas tree in front of the City Hall is a "real" one, I do not doubt for a moment my ordinary capacity to discriminate between genuine and, say, plastic pine trees. Neither do I doubt such a capacity when I begin to consider the possibility that I may be seeing a mirage while driving on an empty desert highway. And so, if one intends to "refute" Descartes by bringing up against him the inherently special and limited scope of doubt generated by the ordinary cases of perceptual illusion,[1] one is simply retracing the steps of Descartes's own reasoning.

The point can be put in even sharper terms. Far from overthrowing the commonsensical view with his analysis of sensory illusions, Descartes undercuts the skeptic's hope of using the existence of such illusions as sufficient grounds for attacking our commonsensical beliefs. For if the confusion between an illusion and a veridical perception occurs only under unusual and atypical circumstances, then by relying upon what we have learned from our senses under normal circumstances we can successfully weed out illusions and deceptions from our sensory experiences. For example, by recalling what I have learned about the colors of objects when I was not sick with jaundice I can come to see that I am being misled by my senses today when—struck with that illness—I perceive my surroundings as if tinted in yellow. By relying upon a background of perceptual certainty while stepping back from my immediate perceptual experience, I can thus correct the latter with the aid of the former, and I can adjust my beliefs accordingly. It is true, of course, that in Descartes's view the sensory evidence turns out to be no evidence at all; thus the data of the senses have to be repudiated as a class. But this position, whatever its merits, is not arrived at by the argument from illusions. Taken all by itself, the argument can at best make us more suspicious about the senses; but even this is at once compensated for by the vindication of all percpetual beliefs acquired and tested under normal circumstances.

The case of dreaming while believing himself to be awake pre-

sents Descartes with a more serious challenge than the case of sensory illusions. For during the dream experience one may falsely
believe oneself to be under normal and optimal conditions of sensory
awareness: "How often has it happened to me that in the night I
dreamt that I found myself in this particular place, that I was dressed
and seated near the fire, whilst in reality I was lying undressed in
bed!" (HR, I, 145–146). Thus the case of dreaming takes us one
step further along the path we have entered with the examination of
sensory illusions, and, this time, the path definitely seems to be
leading to skeptical conclusions. For if we can be so easily misled
into believing ourselves to be under conditions of normal perception,
then the very background of perceptual certainty we ordinarily rely
upon in order to detect illusions will be of no use to us at all. And so,
any hope of correcting our senses will have to be abandoned.

But the joy of the skeptic may still be premature. For are we sure
that the doubt born out of our acquaintance with dream illusions can
be generalized? Do we have all the steps needed to arrive at the
skeptical conclusion?

In order to answer these questions we first must bring into sharp
focus just what it is that happens in the cases where we indisputably
do confuse dream images with veridical perceptions; we shall then
be in a better position to see whether the inference from such cases
to the general skeptical conclusion can be justified.

Now the new and the particularly alarming quality of the dream
experience is a radical modification in the status of our thinking—
in sharp contrast with what happens in the state of a mere sensory
illusion. In effect, the latter never has a complete grip upon me. I
can reasonably hope to separate sensory illusions from veridical
perceptions, since my critical faculties are never totally enclosed
and caught up within a particular sensory experience. While I am
awake, my thought and my memory transcend the boundaries of
my perceptual here and now; I can therefore critically examine my
immediate perceptual experience by bringing to bear upon it my
theoretical knowledge and my acquaintance with cases of similar
experiences I have had in the past. Due to this freedom of my
thought and of my memory I can—if I am careful enough—succeed in identifying and correcting an illusion and thus in eliminat-
ing its impact upon my beliefs. But I can do no such a thing while
dreaming, for my thought and my memory are then part and parcel
of the dream experience itself. I cannot step back, as it were, from

the dream images I am having in order to subject them to corrections and verifications. This is why my past attempts to verify and check a dream experience *while having it* have all ended up in a failure. There were indeed many cases when, puzzled by some unusual features of my experience, I hastened to reassure myself by the thought that I was not dreaming. At the moment of entertaining that thought I was firmly convinced that I was awake. And yet, the strength of my conviction notwithstanding, I soon discovered that I *was* dreaming after all. In cases like these, the thought that I was not dreaming was, as it turned out, an element of the very same dream experience which I felt I could certify as a genuine perception. It seems, then, that I can be easily misled into believing myself to be under the conditions of normal and optimal perception by simply thinking in a dream that I am under such conditions.

Can we generalize this doubt? We have said nothing so far that would allow us to do so. The new element introduced in the total picture is the peculiar status of the dreamer's thought. The dreamer's thought is fully immersed in his experiences—it cannot disentangle itself from images and representations in order to verify them. All of this can be granted without any threat of skepticism ever materializing itself. For the skeptic now has to convince us that there are no marks through which we could discriminate between, on the one hand, acts of thought that are (as in dreaming) totally imprisoned by the subject's images and representations and, on the other hand, such acts of thought in which we can step back from our immediate experiences in order to check their veracity. Now our obvious failure to detect such marks in some cases—that is, our failure to sometimes detect the difference between an act of thought immersed in an experience and an act of thought capable of stepping back from an experience—does not yet warrant the general mistrust of our ability to do so in other cases.

Someone could be tempted to reply that sufficient reasons have already been offered to at least undercut the trust in our ability to perform such successful discriminations in the case of our present experiences. In effect, I come to realize that my thought of not being immersed in a dream was itself part of a dream *when I wake up*. But then my only hope of ever successfully identifying this or that thought "I am not dreaming now" as being itself a dream illusion would have to depend upon some version of a *retrospective* checking of my experiences. And this is all the skeptic wants us to grant him, for he can then argue successfully that the experience from which we do our retrospective checking can itself be checked only retrospectively; the same restriction can then be applied to our next checkpoint and so on indefinitely. From this it will follow that at no point of our mental history can we be sure we are not dreaming—and this is precisely what the skeptic wants us to assent to.

However, I do not believe that Descartes allows for only such retrospective checking, nor do I believe that such a supposition could even be made compatible with the broader framework of his theory. Descartes, I am going to argue, is and must be firmly committed to the view that at least some of our perceptual experiences can be clearly distinguished from dream images at the very moment when we are having them. In other words, the mere occurrence of dream illusions does not give us sufficient grounds to doubt the veracity of all of the first-person present-tense reports "I am not dreaming now." For let us suppose for a moment that Descartes would want us to rely only upon retrospective tests. We would then have to confront immediately the following choice:

1. If, when having the experience E' while casting a retrospective glance upon my past experience E, I *can* tell successfully that E was in fact a genuine perception and not a dream image, then E' cannot itself be a dream illusion (for then my entire assessment of E would be worthless), and, in this case, I do know that I am not dreaming at least in E'.

2. If at no point of my mental history do I truly know that I am not dreaming, then at no point of my mental history can I be sure that I am performing a genuine retrospective verification; for all I know, I could still be *dreaming* of myself as being in the state of performing such a verification.

Now a quick glance at the conjunction of (1) and (2) yields at once the following conclusion: either it makes sense to rely upon retrospective checking of my experiences, but then it must be the case that I am in principle capable of discriminating between dreams and perceptions in my present experiences; or it is indeed the case that I can never know whether my present experience is a dream illusion or a veridical perception, but then I can never rely upon the method of retrospective verification.

But, one could object, the skeptic could still come out winning by simply refusing to be locked into the alternative of (1) and (2). He could be quite happy with a very modest claim that it is at least *logically possible* for someone to be in a position where he cannot know if he is dreaming or genuinely perceiving. To put it in the first person: I do not need to know as a *matter of fact* that in some specific experiences I mistook dreaming for perceiving; what is quite sufficient to justify the skeptical conclusion is the very thought that it is *logically possible* for me to be in a state where a dream experience is indistinguishable from a veridical perception, for it then seems to follow that I cannot know if I am not in such a state right now.[2]

However, let us take a closer look at this suggestion. How do I know that it is even "logically possible" for a dream image to be indistinguishable from a perception? Surely, this cannot follow from some arbitrary definitions of the concepts of dreaming and perceiving. The philosopher's concepts of dreaming and perceiving must reflect his acquaintance with what dreaming and perceiving are in fact. It is only on the grounds of his familiarity with such experiences that the philosopher has the right to advance his skeptical claims. And even if we were to permit the skeptic to back up his arguments with the experiences of other people ("*X* has told me that he was once unable to tell the difference between dream images and perceptions . . . , etc."), our magnanimity would in no way change the nature of the case, for we would then have to assume that at least the persons whose reports the skeptic is relying upon were themselves genuinely acquainted with cases of confusion between dreams and veridical perceptions. And so, in order to know that it is (even) logically possible to confuse the state of dreaming with the state of perceiving, it is necessary to know of a case in which such confusion did take place.

How *does* one come to know that one was simply dreaming while being firmly convinced of being awake? Descartes is quite clear on this point: "when he has awakened he will easily detect his error" (HR, II, 78). To take this claim seriously we must assume that the subject knows he is definitely not asleep at the moment he is "detecting his error"; we must assume that he is speaking from the position of someone who knows he is awake. And this is another way of saying that his identification of some of his past states as states of being asleep is taking place against the background of states in which he knows himself to be awake. It is possible, of course, to complicate the case. It is possible to imagine a situation in which I would be firmly convinced that I am awake, that I am casting a careful retrospective glance upon my previous experience, that I am recognizing it as a mere dream, while in fact I would only be dreaming of myself as doing all these things. Thus my recognition of the (past) experience E as a dream would itself belong to the (present) dream experience E'. It is even possible to strain our imagination one step further and to envision a subject who is dreaming in the next experience E'' as well, even while being firmly convinced that he has finally hit upon the firm rock of the waking life. But this series of illusions and misidentifications must stop at some point, for I cannot find myself in situations of confusing dreams and perceptions without finding or having found myself in situations where I knew no such confusion was taking place. To restate this final conclusion: for me to know that it is logically possible that I find myself caught up within a dream while believing myself to be awake I must take for granted my general ability to successfully discriminate between dreams and perceptions.

Are we then to simply ignore Descartes's warning (HR, I, 146) about the *lack* of "certain indications" capable of setting a firm boundary line between dreaming and being awake? But this is precisely what Descartes himself does in the *Sixth Meditation*! As it turns out, there *is* a mark special to our waking experiences—and that is simply their coherence with our entire mental history: "at present I find a very notable difference . . . inasmuch as our memory can never connect our dreams one with the other, or with the whole course of our lives, as it unites events which happen to us while we are awake" (HR, I, 199).

An objection—Hobbes's objection (HR, II, 78)—comes immediately to one's mind. Couldn't I be dreaming that my memory succeeds in establishing coherent links between a particular experience and the rest of my mental history? If, as seems to be quite possible, the thought of such coherence can itself be part of a dream, then what right do I have to believe that my awareness of coherence in my perceptions is to be trustworthy?

Let us note immediately Descartes's unequivocal reply to Hobbes: "One who dreams cannot effect a real connection between what he dreams and the ideas of past events, though he can dream that he does connect them" (ibid.). The doubt generated by the mistaken application of the coherence criterion cannot be generalized: when I sometimes merely dream that I notice coherent links in my experiences I soon ("when he has awakened," as Descartes puts it in the same passage) come to detect and correct my mistake. Since the concepts of detecting and correcting mistakes do imply that I am awake while doing the appropriate corrections it cannot be the case that I am *never* sure whether (*a*) I only dream of this or that experience as being coherent with my mental history, or whether (*b*) I have a genuine waking knowledge of such coherence. Once again, it is of course possible that I may *sometimes* merely dream of myself as detecting and correcting my earlier—and erroneous— assessment of my experience *E* as being coherent with the overall body of memories I have of my entire past history. But, again, this series must come to an end. For if I *know*—and Descartes tells me I do—that in some cases I had only a dream illusion concerning a particular experience's coherence with the rest of my history, I must *also* know—and Descartes tells me this too—that in other cases I had a genuine knowledge of such coherence.

Couldn't I *always* be mistaken in believing myself to have the knowledge that my experiences fit into a coherent pattern? Perhaps I could. But let us grasp clearly the consequences of such a supposition. If at *any* stage of my mental life I could have but a dream illusion of detecting coherence in my experiences, then either (*a*) I would have to (sometimes) know that I am awake *independently* of any reliance upon the coherence criterion, or (*b*) (in case I should continue to depend upon the coherence criterion) my entire mental life could be nothing but a mere dream illusion. Now Descartes is not oblivious to this second possibility, but he is relying upon some very special considerations to make it a real menace to us. In effect, the thought that our *entire* mental life may be a "coherent dream" undercuts at once our ordinary concepts of dreaming, perceiving, being awake and so on. Since the state of being awake and genu- inely perceiving is ordinarily identifiable by the criterion of co- herence, the suspension of the latter destroys our ability to under- stand *what counts as* a state of truly perceiving. The difficulty is not limited to this or that particular experience, but it concerns the task of grasping the difference between perceiving and dreaming "as such," or "in general." Were we to try to ignore this difficulty, we would end up by describing the world with the aid of a conceptual scheme devoid of any distinction between dreaming and perceiv- ing. The mere occurrence of dream illusions could never justify our adoption of such an unusual conceptual scheme. On the contrary, by focusing upon cases where we are in fact misled into considering a state of dreaming as a state of being awake, Descartes's analysis reinforces the dependability of the coherence criterion as such. For, as we saw, our failure in some cases to identify a mental state as a dream image adds additional support to the soundness of our belief in being awake in other cases.

On the other hand, the supposition that we may never know if we are in fact perceiving and not dreaming *is* entirely meaningful to Descartes. Only this supposition has nothing to do with the occurrence, now and then, of dream illusions and everything to do with the possibility that we might be at the mercy of an omnipotent and evil spirit: "How can you be certain that your life is not a perpetual dream and that all that you imagine you learn by means of your senses is not as false now as it is when you sleep? More particularly as you have learned that you have been created by a superior Being to whom as omnipotent it would not have been more difficult to make us such as I have described than as such you believe yourself to be?" (HR, I, 314).

Descartes has now destroyed our confidence in our natural ability to weed out dream illusions with the aid of the coherence criterion, for he has cast doubt upon that very criterion itself through his hypothesis of an "evil demon" or "deceiving god."[3] As long as the hypothesis is not refuted, the criterion is not to be relied upon. Thus an atheist may still go on using it, but since he cannot prove that he is not being misled by a powerful evil spirit he has no *right* to claim that he is succeeding in distinguishing between dreaming and being awake (HR, II, 78). Furthermore—and this adds additional weight to our interpretation—when unfolding his main argument in the *First Meditation* Descartes does not suspend his assent to perceptual cognition in general until after he has introduced the hypothesis of a powerful evil spirit bent on confusing us.[4] Such a disposition of the main argument is not a matter of chance. For, first, the mere fact of dream illusions occurring (sometimes) in our lives cannot take us, all by itself, to the conclusion that in *no* case can we be sure of being able to tell the difference between an illusion and a veridical perception. And, second, such a generalized skeptical conclusion demands the suspension of the very criteria with the aid of which we normally tell the difference between dreaming and perceiving: the skeptic implies that no matter how carefully we may handle such criteria with our native cognitive powers, no matter how "normal" and "optimal" our sensory awareness may seem to us at the time, we are in principle doomed to fail, since we are relying upon defective concepts. And those concepts are not defective because they are "materially false," that is, unclear and confused. Our criterion of coherence, as well as our concept of waking experiences as coherent, are entirely clear and distinct, for we can securely fall back upon them in the *Sixth Meditation,* when all clear and distinct ideas have been vindicated. But they have been vindicated and saved for us only because we have gone beyond the hypothesis of evil demon.

Let us conclude. Taken by itself, the analysis of dreams represents a radicalization of the line of thought first introduced with Descartes's assessment of the damage done to our knowledge by sensory illusions. The dream argument—if this is the proper term for Descartes's examination of dream illusions—makes us still more suspicious of our perceptual knowledge, but it does not undercut the latter as a whole. By taking into account the possibility of confusing a veridical perception with a sensory illusion, I came to understand that I should rely upon my senses only under normal and typical conditions of their operation. Nothing *further* was to be learned from the argument from illusion. Were I to suspend, on its strength alone, my confidence in perception as a whole, I would be doing something Descartes didn't hesitate to label "extravagant." The dream argument takes us one step further. Descartes now intends to warn us against succumbing too quickly to the comforting thought of being in a normal and typical sensory state. He admonishes us to back up that thought with his coherence criterion. But, again, the doubt takes us no further. It cannot be generalized. While hunting for incoherences in my experiences so as to be able to weed out dream illusions, I do not for a moment cast doubt upon the basic coherence of the main body of my perceptual beliefs. To undercut perception as a whole much more is needed than what the argument from dreams could ever yield. And this is why, when pressed by Hobbes to spell out the real novelty of his view (HR, II, 60), Descartes severely limits the impact of his entire reflexion upon dreams and sensory illusions by reducing its function to the one of a pedagogical and preparatory exercise.[5] The full-blown skepticism will not emerge until we have entertained and drawn conclusions from the hypothesis of evil demon.

But we still have some terrain to cover before our encounter with the evil demon can take place. In a last attempt to escape the looming threat of total doubt Descartes tries to invest his hopes in the evidence of "some other objects yet more simple and more universal, which are real and true" (HR, I, 146) and make up the domains of such sciences as arithmetic and geometry.

This new hope is born out of Descartes's closer examination of dream images. In effect, the unreal content of a dream is a combination of elements which seem to be borrowed from veridical perception. Not unlike a painter's imagination—which often utilizes ordinary shapes, sizes, and colors in order to produce pictures of sirens and satyrs—the imagination of a dreamer produces representations that, while illusory in themselves, are composed of simple items borrowed from perception. Hence if we are careful enough to assent only to truths about such "simple" elements— that is, about representations that are not concatenations of other representations—we may find ourselves in the possession of a rule allowing us to stay away from the entire area of possible errors and deceptions.

It could seem at first that the argument, when so stated, produces the exact opposite of what we said was Descartes's view of the evil demon hypothesis. For if we are told to refrain from assenting to any complex idea on the grounds that its very complexity can be an occasion for error, then it seems as if Descartes was in a position to undercut our entire perceptual knowledge, without relying upon the evil demon hypothesis, simply by putting some more flesh upon the bare bones of his dream argument. In effect, Descartes's present move can easily be read as representing the following reasoning: (1) any complex representation can, due to its complexity alone, turn out to be a dream image; (2) perception is always complex (we never perceive simple elements; for example, we do not perceive some punctual, instantaneous flashes of red, but always a red surface, or a red cube, etc.); hence (3) it is possible that all of my perceptions (including the present one) may in fact be dream images. And so it is at least *logically* possible that I may find myself in situations where I am dreaming while being convinced of having a veridical perception. Nothing more is needed to justify skeptical conclusions.

But this interpretation of Descartes's new interest in dream illusions is off target. All Descartes has said so far is that the complex nature of our representations is the necessary condition of deception; he has not said, nor did he intend to say, that the same condition is also *sufficient* to induce someone into taking a dream for a perception. To put it differently, from the fact that it is *logically possible* for every complex representation to be a mere dream image, it does not follow at all that we do not know *as a matter of fact* that some such representations are genuine perceptions. Let us restate one more time the point we have already made while analyzing the main body of Descartes's dream argument. For me to entertain the logical possibility of confusing the state of dreaming with the state of perceiving, I must as a matter of fact know of some cases in my mental history where such confusion did take place. But I cannot explain how I came to know of such cases if I don't assume that in other cases I was perfectly capable of correctly discriminating between dreaming and perceiving. No generalization is warranted here: both my concept of perception and my belief in having genuinely perceived in some situations are still left intact, and they still provide the background against which deceptions (actual or possible) are recognized and identified as such.

What, then, *is* the purpose of Descartes's new approach to dream illusions? The purpose is made clear to us by Descartes himself: "whether I am awake or asleep, two and three together always form five, and the square can never have more than four sides, and it does not seem to be possible that truths so clear and apparent can be suspect of any falsity [or uncertainty]" (HR, I, 147). To put the same point differently: the certainty of mathematical propositions is such that it will not diminish "whether [mathematical ideas] are actually existent or not" (ibid.).

I think we must here take Descartes's words quite literally and at their face value. His new argument is purported to show a much greater resistance of mathematical truths to doubt; Descartes is now indicating to us that the propositions of (at least) pure mathematics are in effect logically independent of all perceptual cognition. But it is important to notice that the argument is *not* purported to supply sufficient reasons for repudiating all perceptual cognition. Mathematics would escape doubt *even if* perception was entirely unreliable; but this consideration is not meant to justify the claim that perception *is* entirely unreliable.

Now the reason why the truths of pure mathematics are logically independent of all perceptual beliefs emerges clearly from Descartes's talk about those "simple and universal natures" mathematics is supposed to be dealing with. For those simple and universal natures—Descartes was expounding on them already in the *Rules for the Direction of the Mind*—do not make up the *content* of our knowledge but its necessary *form*. And this difference will explain why the kind of doubt that undercuts our trust in the former does not affect the certainty of the latter.

In the *Rules* (HR, I, 41) Descartes divides these formal components of our knowledge into three classes—they are either spiritual, or material, or mixed. The first class is composed of concepts that make up the form of our knowledge of minds. We shall find here such concepts as those of knowledge, doubt, ignorance, volition, and so on. Without assuming that we know such concepts and can apply them successfully, we would have no cognitive access to *our own* mental life; we would not be able to identify and classify even the most elementary kinds of mental experience. The second class of our universal concepts refers to certain features common to all physical objects: Descartes gives examples of figure, extension, and movement. Finally, there are also some universal concepts which apply across the board to both minds and bodies. These are the ideas of pure mathematics as well as the concepts of existence, unity, duration, "and the like" (ibid.). Since "no knowledge is at any time possible of anything beyond those simple natures and . . . their combination with each other" (HR, I, 43), it becomes clear why, in the *Meditations,* Descartes will attach such great importance to those simple and universal natures' resistance to doubt. For those "natures" are for us the conditions of the possibility of any knowledge whatsoever.[6] Our knowledge of minds and bodies is processed by a conceptual scheme of which those "natures" are the central components. Were *they* to be undercut by the skeptic, we would have lost not simply this or that kind of knowledge but our very ability to know anything at all. To be sure, this is precisely where Descartes intends ultimately to take us. He means his doubt to be a *total* one. Right on the first page of the *Meditations* he announces his purpose as being nothing less than the overthrow of *all* of his beliefs and opinions. The final station of his journey will be the one where the initial question "What can be true?" will have been answered by the resounding "Perhaps nothing at all" (HR, I, 149). But he can get to that final station only if he can find reasons to doubt not this or that kind of knowledge but our very ability to know anything. And such a doubt, if it can be supported at all, will have to be supported by a sustained attack upon the form of knowledge itself. The kinds of reasons to doubt we have seen deployed so far are insufficient to produce such a doubt. As we saw earlier, neither the dream argument nor the argument from illusion are broad enough to undercut my confidence in my ability to know *as such*. Not only do I continue to rely upon my conceptual scheme while detecting dreams and illusions, but even when I do confuse a dream with a perception I don't have the slightest reason to doubt the soundness of that conceptual scheme itself. Nothing has happened so far to the equations of mathematics, or to the concepts of duration, extension, and so on. On account of their simplicity and universality the evidence I detect in those ideas is so strong and compelling that, in order to suspend my assent to them, I would first have to doubt the objective validity of the very criteria of evidence. Only the hypothesis of evil demon can produce a doubt that goes so far.

I shall now discuss this hypothesis in more detail.

When, in the course of deploying his skeptical moves in the *First Meditation* Descartes finally begins to consider the possibility of being deceived by an evil demon, his dry language takes on unexpectedly lively colors. Not only is the demon "malicious," "very powerful," and "very cunning," but he also "employs his whole energies" and "ingenuity" to deceive me "constantly" (HR, I, 148, 150). This vivid picture has a definite function to perform: it is meant to impress upon the reader a sense of *total powerlessness and vulnerability*. Everything is taken care of by Descartes: the intentions and capabilities of the demon are spelled out in such detail as to undercut any confidence one may still put in one's native cognitive powers. And this is the crucial step on Descartes's path toward total doubt. It is only now, after considering the evil demon hypothesis, that Descartes will think he has sufficient grounds for generalizing his doubt (HR, I, 149). For how could he now avoid such a grim perspective? If he might be exposed to the manipulations of a powerful evil spirit against whom he has no defenses, then all of his beliefs, and indeed his very standards and criteria for examining those beliefs, might turn out to be so many deceptive ideas planted in his mind by the ever-present demon.

Could we generate the universal doubt with the aid of something *less* extreme than the evil demon hypothesis? Descartes himself (HR, I, 147) suggests one such possibility: my doubt could be generalized through the realization of the mere *imperfection* of my nature. In effect, if the cause of my being is imperfect and I am not, therefore, perfect myself, then the very limitations of my nature ought to be sufficient to make me wonder about the soundness of my beliefs and standards of evidence.

But I think we can say quite safely that there were good reasons for Descartes's *not* having pursued that possibility as eagerly as he did pursue his hypothesis of the evil demon. For if I am merely limited—and not purposefully deceived by a spirit against whom I can build no defenses—then I can still hope to avoid error by accepting my limits and by not allowing my will to roam free, only assenting to propositions that my limited understanding can grasp clearly and distinctly. Such is, in effect, Descartes's own doctrine from the *Fourth Meditation*. If I acknowledge the limits of my intellect and if I tame my will accordingly, I shall have a firm rule for avoiding error (HR, I, 178). Error is not at all due to some alleged "defect in our nature" (HR, I, 234), and since our nature is by all means a limited one it follows that error cannot stem from our limitation alone. A stronger reason is needed to generate the total doubt Descartes aims at. I must show why I could be deceived even if my cognitive powers were operating at their (however limited) optimal level. It is for this reason that Descartes's excursion into "demonology" is essential to the success of his methodical skepticism.

Let us then take the human intellect in its optimal state, that is, when we entertain some ideas whose clarity and distinctness is so great and so indisputable that we can find no reasons to suspend our assent to them. Now, clarity and distinctness are the marks of evidence, while evidence is the mark of truth. There exists, then, a body of propositions—axioms of mathematics are one example dear to Descartes—whose truth cannot be doubted by us. But the evil demon hypothesis will make us doubt even such truths, since it will undercut the objective validity of what counts as evident to us. We will not be able to escape that predicament, Descartes argues (HR, I, 178), until we have found a secure anchorage for our knowledge in the veracity of God, *"fondement de toute certitude humaine."*[7] As long as we are surrounded by the darkness spread by the evil demon, we may very well grasp a proposition as endowed (due to its clarity and distinctness) with unshakable *evidence*, and yet we will still have to refrain from considering that proposition as *true:* ''if we did not know that all that is in us of reality and truth proceeds from a perfect and infinite Being, however clear and distinct were our ideas, we should not have any reason to assure ourselves that they had the perfection of being true'' (HR, I, 105). This distinction between a proposition's unshakable evidence to our intellect and its objective truth is so important that without it Descartes's own way of deploying philosophical arguments would collapse. Let us take one crucial example: the distinctness of mind and body imposes itself as evident already in the *Second Meditation,* that is, long before the proof of God's veracity is offered, but we will have to wait until we can justifiably depend upon such veracity in order to attribute to that evidence the status of an objective truth (HR, I, 137; II, 101–102). For, as Descartes was warning us at the very beginning of the *Meditations* (HR, I, 140), if we are to be certain that mind is indeed really distinct from the body, we must know not only that we conceive this clearly and distinctly to be the case, but, far more important, we must know that what we clearly and distinctly conceive to be the case is also true—and this is something we cannot know until we are certain of the divine guarantee underlying our clear and distinct ideas.

Let us repeat this one more time: since clarity and distinctness are, for Descartes, marks of epistemic evidence, the doubt cast upon them by the hypothesis of evil demon means nothing short of the total destruction of our evidences' claim to objective truth. There may be nothing wrong per se with a clear and distinct proposition; thus, when I assent to some simple axiom of mathematics its simplicity and transparence will give me no special reason to think I may be wrong in considering the axiom to be true. Here, at least, there is no danger of committing an error in calculations, or of forgetting a step in a proof, and so on. The utter simplicity of the axioms allows me to take them in, as it were, in one mental act of intuition with all the clarity and distinctness required. And yet, as long as I have not ruled out the evil demon hypothesis I have no right to attribute to my evidences any reference to the order of things. For how do I know if my unshakable conviction of the objective truth of p—which I grasp so clearly and so distinctly at least while attending to it mentally—is not itself a product of the evil demon's manipulation? How do I know if my intellect does not constantly lead me into deceptions in those very moments when I grasp something with the utmost clarity and distinctness? If the evil demon is behind all of my beliefs, then my very rationality itself, with all its standards and criteria, turns out to be unreliable as the instrument of the discovery of truth. I must thus suspend not simply this or that belief (or class of beliefs) upon which I can cast some doubt with my own cognitive powers, but I must destroy my confidence in those very powers themselves.

There is another way of putting Descartes's point. What the evil demon hypothesis casts doubt upon is not the soundness of this or that way in which I apply my concepts but the soundness of my entire conceptual scheme. For example, since I am now at the junction of the argument where clarity and distinctness become suspect, I lose the very criterion for telling the difference between perceptions and dreams. My very *concept* of what defines and marks off perceptions from dream images—the ''coherence'' of perceptions—is now undercut and rendered meaningless. As of now, the problem is not that I may wrongly classify a dream image as a veridical perception but that my right to talk about any objectively valid difference between dream images and perceptions of material objects has been taken away from me. Since the criterion of coherence has lost its power, for all I know my entire way of talking about objects as independent of my perceptions of them may very well be entirely misleading and so I may now begin to wonder, as Descartes does, if my entire life is not a dream.

The scholastic terminology Descartes adopts to describe the position he is in at the stage of the total doubt proves to be well suited to his purposes. Let us look at the benefit he derives from employing the concept of ''objective reality.'' With its aid, he can continue to attribute to his ideas a representative quality: the ideas' ''objective reality'' depends upon the perfection of their *ideata,* and so the ideas are still to be seen as representing their *ideata.* At the same time, he can avoid the commitment to the actual existence of those *ideata.* The objective reality of our idea of a horse is measured by the degree of perfection attributed to the animal represented by the idea; but at the stage of methodical skepticism we have now reached, we do not yet know if what our ideas represent exists independently of them. What is now at issue for us is not the relatively simple task of sorting out true and false judgments about things we all posit as actually existing but the task of examining the ontological status of the entire framework within which we posit certain things (rocks, trees, material objects, etc.) as real and *then* go on advancing our judgments about them. In conducting this examination, we must proceed by considering "the ideas only as certain modes of . . . thoughts, without trying to relate them [as we do in judgments] to anything beyond" (HR, I, 160). Suppose we take the idea of a body—the idea of an extended entity existing independently of our perceptions. We do not know, so far, if that idea is a sound one in the sense of telling us something about the way things are. The idea lays a representative *claim* upon us, for it does have an objective reality, and so it points out toward a certain kind of *ideata*. But this claim is as yet unsupported; we do not have the right to assume that such *ideata* as are implied by the idea of a body are in fact items in the furniture of the world. We are thus in a situation where we not only must refrain from identifying this or that item as falling under the concept of a body but where we have suspended the right to apply such a concept altogether. If and when we are reassured that an idea X not only claims to but does in fact represent some domain of the world, we will acquire the right to use that idea in our judgments about things; the judgments will then be true or false depending on whether we will have identified or misidentified an item as belonging to the class of X's.

Let us summarize the outcome of our analysis. Descartes's methodical skepticism does not emerge until the evil demon hypothesis unveils to us *the powerlessness and the vulnerability of our condition.* Total doubt—and this is the sort of doubt Descartes is bent on achieving—is not born out of frustrations and failures of our ordinary epistemic practices. On the contrary, as Descartes himself was well aware, and as he demonstrated time and again, any critical examination of knowledge conducted from within the perspective of the ordinary patterns of life and thought will inevitably lead to the vindication of a background of ordinary concepts, beliefs, attitudes, and so on. To undercut this background, the skeptic must be able to attack not just some special area of the ordinary attitude but that attitude *as a whole.* And for this reason the hypothesis of evil demon is indispensable to Descartes. *After* we have adopted that hypothesis, we will be able to generate the attitude of total doubt by focusing upon the ordinary illusions as well. If I sometimes mistake a dream image for a perception, and if I *also* think I am at the mercy of the evil demon, *then* I cannot be sure that in other cases—even in those cases where I am at my best as a knower—I do not fall prey to similar deceptions. But let us not forget what supplies the rule allowing us to achieve the generalization of the doubt. The rule cannot be posited independently of the evil demon hypothesis. It is not some case of mistaken identification of a dream image as a perception that allows us to pass from partial and special doubt to the suspicion that we might be deceived "in principle." It is the evil demon hypothesis that does this for us, for it brings us face-to-face with our fundamental powerlessness in the world. As long as we have no reason to suspend the reliance upon our native cognitive powers, the state of universal doubt cannot emerge. Every obstacle and frustration—every deception and illusion—will only provide an additional stimulus for the victorious exercise of our cognitive powers as we proceed to separate truths from errors. The evil demon hypothesis puts a brutal end to this success story, for the evil demon hypothesis makes us doubt in principle the reliability of our native cognitive powers. Nothing can succeed any more, since the instrument we are relying upon breaks down.

The doubt is now total indeed, but there is also a price to be paid for the overthrow of the ordinary, commonsensical attitude *as a whole*. As we saw, such an overthrow does not and cannot emerge from *within* the ordinary attitude itself. The evil demon hypothesis is brought forth by a supposition which nothing in the ordinary attitude can force or even suggest, and which therefore cannot be evolved out of that attitude. The state of total doubt is produced by a view—the philosopher's view—that is entirely alien to the attitude of common sense. Hence the man of common sense may easily avenge himself upon the philosopher. He may—and undoubtedly will—reject the entire investigation of the philosopher as irrelevant to the concerns of ordinary life and thought. He can claim that total doubt is due only to a fanciful and outlandish speculation of the philosopher. In fact, he can go even further: he can refuse not only to believe but even to understand the philosophical discourse. To him, such concepts as "doubt" or "ignorance" have a clear meaning determined by our ordinary practices. In terms of those practices doubt and ignorance are always seen as emerging in specific situations and on account of specific failures of our knowledge. When taken out of this ordinary setting, the concepts of doubt and ignorance lose all their meaning to the man of common sense. For this reason, he will dismiss the entire discourse of the philosopher as a perversion of the ordinary way of speaking. And he will not be surprised to learn that such discourse ends up by developing contradictions and by branching off into incompatible systems of thought.

⌐⟶

Lost by Descartes, the connection between skepticism and the preoccupations of ordinary life reemerges in Heidegger. In what follows, I shall be taking a closer look at Heidegger's theory. But first, an important qualification is called for as there are, in effect, two different levels in Heidegger's overall attempt to come to terms with the issue of skepticism.

Beginning with section 13 of *Being and Time,* a sustained effort is made at overcoming the subject/object dichotomy. This dichotomy is typical of the modern epistemological tradition, and it results, Heidegger argues, in a failure to establish any link between the mental life of the knowing self and the external world the self aims at knowing. In effect, once the self is defined as a bearer of representations (of perceptions, thoughts, images, etc.) set over against the world to be known, there seems to be no way of showing how these representations could ever lead the self to the independent world they are supposed to represent. The epistemologist can perhaps discover some regularities and order in the self's representations, but he is in no position to infer from those marks the existence and the properties of an independent world.

Against *this* form of skepticism Heidegger replies not by advancing a more convincing proof or refutation—he considers the very *need* to come up with such a proof the "scandal of philosophy" (*BT* 249)—but by a series of deflationary moves made possible by his description of human Dasein as being-in-the-world. It turns out as we make our way through *Being and Time* that the epistemologist's picture of the knowing self is in fact parasitic upon and derived from a more basic relationship where human beings are enmeshed in their practical everyday environment which gives all reality to their lives. The impact of the epistemologist's question ("How can I know the independent world if I am directly familiar only with my representations") is undermined by the fact that his entire picture of the self is at odds with the features of the epistemologist's own situation in the world, for he too is a being in the world and he thus relies upon the practices and the vocabularies available in the everyday world in order to raise the very skeptical questions he asks. Or, to put it in

more traditional terms: the reality of the world we live in must be
seen as the condition of possibility of the modern epistemologist's
doubt in that reality. It is possible, then, to present Heidegger's
dissolution of the modern epistemological predicament as consisting
of transcendental arguments,[8] even though the term "transcendental
argument" must be severely qualified when used in interpreting
Heidegger's philosophy.[9]

But this is only the first level in Heidegger's analysis of skepticism. On a deeper level, skepticism cannot be diagnosed away as
a distortion of Dasein's original way of participating in (and being
defined by) the world. For that participation is not sustained by any
order of things; and when the groundlessness of man's entire being
in the world is brought home to him in the experience of anxiety in
the face of death, skepticism reemerges, and it does so in a form in
which it cannot be deflated and dissolved by being shown to result
from a limited and secondary attitude derived from a more fundamental—and radically different—relationship of man and world.
There is a "truth" to this form of skepticism, for the context of
intelligibility defining man's insertion in the world is indeed con-
tingent and not grounded in any foundation. A realization of this
state of affairs breaks down our naive reliance upon the practices
and the vocabularies sustaining our commerce with the world, and
such a breakdown signifies the emergence of an attitude through
which Dasein withdraws its endorsement of not only this or that
belief or class of beliefs but of the entire framework in terms of
which we determine certain beliefs as meaningful and then proceed
to establish their truth or falsity.

We can notice at once some important similarities between Descartes's and Heidegger's final accounts of skepticism. For both Descartes and Heidegger the truly profound motive behind the
skeptical attitude is man's realization (through the evil demon hypothesis or through the anxious encounter with death) of the
powerlessness and the vulnerability of his condition in the world.
We shall be returning to this point and explaining it in more detail
in the course of our examination of Heidegger's position. But—and
this shall be of equal importance to us—the significant differences
between the two philosophers ought not to be ignored either. For in
Heidegger doubt is not—or at least is not meant to be—imported
from outside into commonsensical attitudes. Since the commonsensical attitudes themselves are strategies for dealing with the ines-

capable fact of our powerlessness, a sense of that powerlessness
will never be entirely absent from them. Thus skepticism and common sense must be seen as two different but closely related ways of
responding to the same aspect of the human condition. Furthermore, Heidegger will point out specific items in Dasein's structure
that make possible this link between skeptical detachment and ordinary attitudes. The link is made possible by moods (*Stimmungen*).
Since the mood of anxiety is behind the emergence of skeptical
alienation from the world and since anxiety, its special status notwithstanding, belongs to the same family of attitudes as do ordinary
moods (fear, hope, etc.), the message of the skeptic will not be
entirely alien to the man of common sense. We must now make
clear the nature of this connection between the skeptical and the
ordinary attitudes. We will then be in a position to see if—and to
what extent—Heidegger has succeeded in bridging the gap left
wide open by Descartes.

For Heidegger, moods are only familiar manifestations of our
general capacity to be affected by the world, of our *Befindlichkeit*.
This term—not too happily translated as "state-of-mind"—captures quite well Dasein's fundamental dependency and vulnerability. I am always in a mood, for the conditions I am in are not
indifferent to me. The way in which I let things get through to me
(in fear, in hope, in sadness, etc.) is directly perceivable in my
behavior, but I can also try to spell out to someone "how I feel
about them." I thus express a state of being *affected* by the way
things are, I signal to my interlocutor that they *matter* to me one
way or another, that they do not leave me cold.

But the way things matter to me is entirely different in anxiety
and in ordinary moods. As we stated a moment ago, the experience
of anxiety breaks down naive attachment to the ways of the everyday world. This unique function of anxiety is due essentially to two
of its main components. First, anxiety is a form of *Befindlichkeit*, a
mood, and like all moods it both stems from and reveals man's
fundamental vulnerability in the world. Second—and this is where
anxiety differs from other moods—an individual gripped by anxiety does not turn away from the vulnerability of his condition but is
brought face-to-face with it. Strangely enough, this difference between anxiety and other moods is in fact a mark of their kinship.
For the ordinary moods are simply our ways of coping with anxiety—with that terror seizing us in the face of death (*BT* 295)—by

rechanneling it into the familiar and reassuring mold of the world of
common sense (*BT* 175). We make ourselves (in fear, hope, etc.)
dependent upon things and persons in order to conceal our dependency upon death. We thus gain some sense of security and power,
since we do have some margin of control over items of our world,
while we have no such control at all over the fundamental fact of
our mortality. By becoming emotionally attached to, even enslaved
by, things and persons, we are trying to forget and to forestall our
ultimate enslavement by death. It is not by accident, then, that
Heidegger has words of praise for Pascal (*BT* 178), for his own
theory of moods (affects, passions, feelings, etc., to use the traditional terminology) can well be seen as developing the theme from
Pascal's thoughts on "diversion."[10] Moods are strategies for di-
verting one's attention from the fundamental powerlessness discovered through an anxious realization of one's status as a mortal
creature.

We can see immediately why the ordinary moods—all moods,
that is, except the mood of anxiety—will never be able to lead an
individual onto the path of skepticism. For such moods presuppose
the reality of the public world; all of them are defined by the se-
riousness that they attach to things and persons. The public world
must be taken for granted if an individual is to feel dependent upon
and affected by its items.[11] But to take the public world for granted
is to take for granted all the ordinary practices and beliefs that sustain our relationship to it. Whatever doubt might be generated within the ordinary moods it could never be universalized, for such
moods are all strategies pursued within the public world. Anxiety
alone is capable of bringing about the attitude of universal doubt,
for anxiety alienates me from the public world as a whole.

In effect, an attack of anxiety makes me see the spuriousness of
my attachment to things. I was clinging to them in order to forestall
the ever-present threat of death, but I now realize that the vulnerability and the powerlessness of my entire being in the world are
indeed inescapable. Anxiety teaches me that, for anxiety is not a
mood gripping me on account of some specific threat to this or that
specific aim of mine: "This threatening does not have the character
of a definite detrimentality which reaches what is threatened, and
which reaches it with definite regard to a special factical potentiality-for-being" (*BT* 186). Anxiety is completely indefinite; I can
be overwhelmed by it when there is no real or imaginary threat to

my purposes. Since there is no *specific* threat and since, on the other hand, in anxiety I am anxious about the precariousness and powerlessness of my condition in the world, I must be discovering something about that condition *as such.* I am indeed anxious about my entire being in the world (*BT* 233); I am anxious, for I see that my life is at every moment at the mercy of death—of that ultimate power, against which no defenses can be built.

Since there are no defenses against death's violence against me, the tie between myself and the public world—with all its practices and conceptions—is severed. This world cannot protect me now. It breaks down for me at the very moment that I realize its utter uselessness as a shield against my death. *As I cannot depend upon the public world any more, I cease to take its ways for granted.*

The proposition is entirely universal. *Nothing* in the public world offers me a chance to escape the power of death, and so I suspend my allegiance to all of its ways. It is no longer the case that, thwarted in my immediate desires, I simply retreat from the practical attitude into some form of theoretical reflexion or contemplation. Since the theoretical attitude—be it perceptual, scientific, or philosophical—is just as useless to me in my confrontation with death as is the practical attitude, I am led to suspend the former as well. In Heidegger's terminology: both the world of the ready-to-hand *and* the world of the present-at-hand lose their significance for me (*BT* 231, 393). Neither of them can be relied upon—even the present-at-hand is now revealed only in "an empty *mercilessness*" (*BT* 393; my italics)—for they are both equally unable to give me a secure niche against death.

New light can now be shed on anxiety's difference from ordinary moods. Every "state-of-mind," Heidegger is telling us, has its "understanding" (*BT* 182). This means, first of all, that there are no inarticulate moods; every passion, affection, or feeling is shaped by an interpretation; none of them can be identified independently of how Dasein chooses to express them. In effect, moods have not only affective but cognitive components as well. For example, fear is always fear "of" or "about" something; it has an intentional content, and this content is established by Dasein's choice of goals and purposes. Thus, if I fear about my financial investments it is only because I have assigned to them an important place in my life plan and in the strategies called forth to realize it. Perhaps a person committed to different goals would have greeted the same financial loss with hearty laughter. And so my mood is always defined by goals and purposes within which I have chosen to express it. To be sure, the selection of those goals and purposes is in turn restricted by the mood: "understanding always has its mood" (*BT* 182), says Heidegger. Clearly, if mine is a quiet and fearful way of coping with the burdens of life, then I am not going to join a group of mercenaries bent on overthrowing the government of a faraway country. But this is simply another way of getting at Heidegger's main point: while interdependent, mood and understanding are also irreducible to each other. Taken by itself, then, a mood is nothing more than a vague task, a problem, which it is up to me to solve by taking over some possibilities laid out for me in the public world.

Now, I have no such choice open to me when the mood at issue is anxiety. Or, to be more precise, the only choice I still have is how to play the role already imposed upon me by the power of death: the role of a mortal being. While I can freely shape the meaning of a fearful or a hopeful mood, I cannot shape the meaning of anxiety—I can only try to conceal it, to cover it up—for anxiety reveals to me the utmost powerlessness of my meaning-giving activity as a whole.

The theory of moods as escape strategies of a Dasein unable to come to terms with its own powerlessness in the face of death allows us to account for the persistent "objectivity" of affective qualities of things and persons. This objectivity is a stumbling block to any merely *intentional* account of our affective life. To be sure, such an account represents an undeniable progress over psychologism; this is why Heidegger shows appreciation (*BT* 178) for Scheler's pioneering work in the field of intentional analysis of passions and emotions. One thing is clear in any case: moods are not "inner states" of some private, isolated self, for they are our ways of comporting ourselves toward the world. To be shaken by fear is not to be struck by some mental event but to discover, all of a sudden, a frightening and threatening face of the world. However, with the aid of the intentional analysis alone we will not be able to account for the conjunction of the two following facts: (1) it is only through the human attitudes and stances that the world is invested with affective qualities; "in itself," the world is neither frightening, nor pleasant, etc.; and (2) the affective qualities are *perceived* by us as qualities of things and persons and not as precipitates of our own attitudes. It will not do, to resolve this difficulty, to appeal to some hypothetical mechanisms of unconscious projection that would explain how an individual can fall into the "illusion" of imputing to things his own affective interpretations of them. Quite apart from the obvious difficulty in establishing the existence and the mode of operation of such a projective mechanism—Hume's theory of imagination comes immediately to one's mind, and so too do all of its shortcomings—we would be hard-pressed to account for its persistent strength in the life of even most critically minded individuals. Why do we cling so strongly to this "illusory" objectivity of affective qualities? Heidegger's theory meets the objection head-on. Man must succumb to the common-sensical illusion of objectivity of affective qualities, since he cannot afford to see through the strategy behind his own activity of investing the world with them. For that strategy is the strategy of escaping from the inescapable power of death. Were I to unmask that strategy I would indeed be able to rediscover the man-made status of affective qualities, but I would also be forced to look into the abyss of my total powerlessness in the face of death.

Suppose, now, that such encounter with the power of death is suddenly forced upon me by anxiety. We have already noted, a moment ago, how anxiety is instrumental in bringing about the emergence of the skeptical attitude. Since the public realm cannot protect me from death's violence, that realm *as a whole* is suddenly perceived as failing me. This is what makes me disenchanted with it, and this is what alienates me from the ordinary patterns of life and belief. The power of death destroys my confidence in the "truths" of the public world. The public practices and interpretations are of no use to me anymore (*BT* 233).

At this point, an objection springs immediately to one's mind: why *should* an individual withdraw his endorsement of the truths of the public world just because that world turns out to be unable to *practically* defend him against death? Why couldn't he at least *think* of his death in terms of the public and publicly available conceptual scheme, thereby only recommitting himself to it? After all, can't I think of my death along the lines of the public discourse? Can't I see my death as, for example, "what we all have to go through in order to rejoin our ancestors?" Or as "a common fate of all living bodies?"

Heidegger's answer to this objection is well known (*BT* 297–

298). Certainly, I can articulate my death within the conceptual scheme I rely upon as a member of the public world. Only I am not thereby talking about *my* death. I now consider myself as merely a member of a class defined by certain common features. My death is brought to a common denominator with the deaths of others. And this way of viewing my death *is* a means of defending myself against it with the aid of the public world. In effect, when so depersonalized by the public discourse, my death becomes at once stripped of its threatening quality; I become tranquilized about it, I now consider it as part and parcel of the ordinary, daily routine. And, of course, like all similar defenses this one too will break down as soon as anxiety unveils to me the true face of my death. At that moment, the security of the public discourse will vanish.

But, one could object still further, is all of this really sufficient to recognize the limits of the public discourse *as such?* Can the doubt be generalized? It seems not. For even if I can find no hope of resisting death's violence within *this* public world I am familiar with from my ordinary life, I can still hope and dream that *some* public realm could protect me against death. To destroy that further hope much more would be needed than the collapse of the public world I happen to be living within.

To refute this possible objection let us note first of all that the sentence we have just written would have made very little sense to Heidegger. I do not "happen" to live in my public world in the sense that I could always freely abandon it "in thought" and imagine myself taking up the practices and the conceptions of another public world. *My* world's understanding of reality is the only understanding *I* have. To advance any other view would be to deny Dasein's inescapable thrownness (*Geworfenheit*). Thus the collapse of practices and vocabularies available in the public world I live in does not leave me free to envision, pick, and choose other vocabularies and ways of interpreting reality; such a collapse signifies the breakdown of the one and only framework of intelligibility within my reach.

Furthermore—and even more important for the purposes of the present study—were we to grant an individual seized by anxiety the ability of adopting "in thought" some alternative vocabulary or conceptual scheme, it would still not follow that such a possibility would be sufficient to eliminate the skeptical attitude as the latter emerges in the individual's encounter with his own death. For it is not the case that I come to view my death as irrevocable because I have discovered that *my* public realm cannot shelter me against it; on the contrary, it is because I have first discovered the ultimateness and the irrevocability of death that my public realm breaks down for me. If death is indeed an individual's ultimate limit—his *"possibility of the impossibility of any existence at all"* (*BT* 307)—then *all* possible public realms are eliminated as candidates for a safe haven for him. Thus, even if someone were to press Heidegger into accepting the terminology of essences, he would still be in a position to refute the entire objection by answering that anxiety reveals to me the unreliability of *any* public realm, the unreliability of publicness "as such."

We can now move closer toward understanding Heidegger's final position on skepticism.

"A sceptic can no more be refuted than the Being of truth can be proved" (*BT* 271). This statement is put forward in the concluding part of Heidegger's analysis of truth in *Being and Time*. It reflects quite well the importance of Heidegger's view of truth as "uncoveredness" (*Entdecktheit*) to the problem of skepticism. Because, as we shall see in a moment, truth is uncoveredness, and because uncoveredness is an item in the structure of Dasein, it is *unnecessary* to ask for a refutation of skepticism: as long as Dasein is, it is "in truth." For the same reason, it would be altogether *impossible* to produce a rational refutation of skepticism. For the very principles of rationality to which one would have to appeal in order to come up with such a refutation are suspended by Dasein's (anxious) realization of its own finitude.

We must now spell out Heidegger's position in more detail. The example Heidegger employs in his analysis (*BT* 260) has by now become a celebrated case: someone with his back turned to the wall makes a true assertion, "the picture on the wall is hanging askew"; our ordinary epistemic standards require that the true assertions be *justified* if they are to count as pieces of knowledge, and so Heidegger moves to explore the "ontological meaning" (*BT* 218) of such justifications ("confirmations") as they are produced in ordinary epistemic practices. Now, the process of such confirmation—for example, the person turns around and looks at the picture—goes directly to the *thing itself*. The person is not, ordinarily, trying to match a "mental image" with a "material object"; he is turning around to take a good look at the picture "just as it is in itself" (*BT*

218). True knowledge, we may say, consists in grasping things in what they *really are*—free of the layers of superficial and disguising presentations—and thus truth and being must belong to the same family of notions (*BT* 213). To have a sense of truth is to have a sense of things being one way or another, that is, a sense of what the world is like and what there is to know. Thus our ordinary practice of making assertions and confirming them does indeed have an *ontological* meaning, for the justification of any ordinary assertion presupposes some form of our commitment to the way things are. When the person looks at the wall in order to confirm the assertions about the picture, he is already committed to a practice and a vocabulary in which such things as pictures, walls, etc., have their proper places. It does not occur to him to entertain any doubts as to whether his talk about pictures and walls is or is not inherently flawed or misleading. He takes for granted both that there are such items and that he is capable of identifying circumstances in which he is in fact perceiving them. It is against the background of such a general commitment that the person will either confirm or disconfirm a particular assertion.[12]

An assertion, we noted, is confirmed when we see that it exhibits things for what they really are. A formal, semantic definition of truth passes over this "phenomenon of truth" (*BT* 262) in which truth appears as uncoveredness. Once we focus our attention upon that—usually ignored—aspect of truth, the latter's connection with Dasein becomes easier to grasp. In a true assertion things must be uncovered for what they really are. But what is to count as "what there really is"? Dasein alone is the key to the puzzle, for it is only in reference to human practices and vocabularies that it makes sense to talk about the way things really are. In taking a stand on what it means to be human, Dasein takes a stand on the meaning of being in general. Or, to put it differently, in committing himself to a certain way of living the human condition man also commits himself to a certain view of what there is and what there is to know. And so the phenomenon of truth—an assertion confirms itself as true when it exhibits things as they really are—turns out to be founded upon Dasein's way of articulating ("disclosing") the world. "Newton's laws, the principle of contradiction, any truth whatever—these are true only as long as Dasein *is*. Before there was any Dasein, there was no truth; nor will there be any after Dasein is no more" (*BT* 269).

The disclosure of the world is not *itself* an epistemic relation. Quite the contrary, it first makes the latter possible. This is why Heidegger views knowledge as a mode of Dasein "founded upon Being-in-the-World" (*BT* 90). In effect, if our words can be hooked onto things, if our cognitions can be matched with their objects, it is only because both poles of the epistemic relation—as well as that relation itself—emerge from Dasein's disclosure of the world. Hence as long as Dasein's disclosure of the world remains intact, doubt can be only local and parochial. It can never swallow up the entire background of perceptual and practical certainties, for these certainties supply the framework for Dasein's disclosure of the world.

Let us pay closer attention to this point. For Heidegger, the disclosing of the world has nothing to do with developing some abstract conception of reality. Being, Heidegger never tires of repeating, is always the being of entities. What this implies for our present concern is something of the following sort: Dasein's sense of what counts as the furniture of the world is dependent upon Dasein's ability to grasp and to recognize some specific items as exemplars of such furniture. For example, if the world I live in is viewed by me as made up of material bodies, then I must be thoroughly familiar with some typical or paradigmatic situations in which my position is taken to be the one of a subject perceiving or manipulating a material body. Should I cast doubt upon my ability to recognize such situations I would have to cast doubt upon the validity of the very *concept* of a material body. Conversely, as long as I endorse such a concept, I can never universalize my doubts. I may, of course, wonder if in *this* particular case what I take to be a tree is in fact a genuine material object and not a sensory illusion. But then, (1) I must have some specific reasons for believing that my present perceptual position departs from the typical cases, and (2) I must be taking for granted that such typical cases are beyond challenge.

The challenge—the skeptical challenge—will be made possible when anxiety discloses to an individual the conditioned, situated character of truth. Since the way things are laid out and articulated by the individual's public world will be of no help to him in coming to terms with the violence of death, the ways of that world will cease to be his ways: he will not take them for granted anymore, as they will have proved themselves entirely useless as defenses against death. By thus discovering the limit of the public world the individual will have understood that the ''truth'' of the former was all shot through with ''untruth.''

Heidegger's talk about untruth has here[13] a fairly precise meaning. The untruth of the public world is due to the *falling* of Dasein (*BT* 264). As man becomes absorbed in the public world, its ways come to be viewed as natural and given. Man sees them as mirroring the natural order of things, or as based on some objective standards of rationality, and so on. And thus a particular way of interpreting the world is suddenly hypostatized into the total picture of reality. A parochial and limited perspective is imposed upon being. This is the original distortion or untruth upon which the public world builds a secure niche for its members. Once an individual loses the sense of that security—once he is brought face-to-face with the threat of his death in the experience of anxiety—he is put in a position where he can grasp the situated and perspectival character of the public interpretation of the world.[14]

Now, if anxiety is what alienates me from the ways of the public world, and if anxiety can grip me even when I do not confront any specific obstacles to any specific goals of mine, then it becomes possible to understand why the skeptical attitude can very well emerge even under the most favorable epistemic conditions. Suppose I am the person who makes the assertion, ''The picture on the wall is hanging askew.'' Taking for granted—as I now do—the practices and the vocabulary of the public world, I can entertain no doubt that I perceive a picture hanging askew on the wall. I feel no need to engage in any additional tests, for my present situation is immediately recognized as conforming to the paradigm cases of genuine perception. But it is just such paradigm cases that my anxiety will challenge. Alienated by anxiety from the public interpretation of the world, I may then begin to wonder whether it makes sense at all to talk about such things as pictures, walls, etc.

Heidegger's final word on skepticism (''A sceptic can no more be refuted than the Being of 'truth' can be proved'') becomes much clearer now. The being of truth cannot be ''proved,'' for the premises and the rules of inference needed to produce such a proof are all suspended by Dasein's discovery of its finitude; for the same reason, there can be no objectively valid refutation of skepticism. On the other hand, the very need to come up with such proofs and refutations stems only from the traditional philosophers' ignorance of man's condition in the world. Once we achieve a grasp of that condition, we shall be able to see that the commitment to truth and the withdrawal into skepticism are both human responses to the task of being in the world. Man is always "in" truth to the extent to which human life defines itself by taking a stand on what it means to be: to be human is to commit oneself to live with a certain sense of what there is and what there is to know. But to be human also means to have the possibility of (anxiously) recognizing this relative character of truth.

We can now spell out in more detail the important similarities and differences between Descartes's and Heidegger's views on skepticism. For both of them, skepticism results from man's awareness of his total powerlessness in the face of a threat to which there is *nothing* he can possibly oppose. All of his ordinary powers and capacities—both practical and cognitive—must be doubted, since they cannot be relied upon to protect him against the violence of, respectively, the evil demon or his own death. For both Descartes and Heidegger, the skeptical attitude is not of an epistemic but of an ontological nature: it expresses man's sense of being vulnerable and exposed in his position in the order of things.

But the differences are at least as significant as are the similarities. For Descartes, the skeptical attitude is not generated by the considerations conducted within the ordinary life. The Cartesian doubt undercuts ordinary life through the adoption of the hypothesis of the evil demon. To a man firmly committed to the practices and the assumptions of the ordinary life, such a doubt must appear artificial and artificially concocted. For all intents and purposes, this man will now reply to the philosopher, I may safely repudiate and ignore the mode of reflection leading to the skeptical attitude. The doubts that *I* confront in ordinary life—and I do sometimes have trouble telling the difference between a perception and a sensory illusion, or between a recollection and a *déjà vu,* etc.—can all be resolved within ordinary life with the aid of my own native powers and capacities. To suspend *in principle* one's confidence in the reliability of these powers and capacities—to assume that they could somehow "go wrong" even while operating at the very peak of their normal performance—would be to make use of language and thought in a way that is both unnecessary and impossible. Such a doubt is indeed unnecessary, for the possibility of evil demon does not appear as a real issue to the ordinary man, preoccupied as he is with specific and definite problems calling for specific and definite uses of his powers and capacities. And the doubt is impossible, for the ordinary life is where all language must ultimately find its source, and so a mode of speaking departing from its natural setting would soon expose itself as a string of meaningless sounds: we couldn't continue to talk about "doubt," "suspension of beliefs," etc., while at the same time severing the connection of such expressions with their natural place in the ordinary life. But the man of ordinary life would have a much harder time in replying along similar lines to Heidegger. For Heidegger's *intention* at least is quite clear at this point: the message of the skeptic is not to be seen as entirely alien to the experience of ordinary life. The man of anxiety holds up to the man of common sense a mirror in which the latter recognizes *his own* concealed face. Since his blind attachment to the ways of the public world was all built upon his own strategy of escaping from the inescapable—from the ever-present threat of death—his puzzlement at the message of the skeptic will be mixed up with a sense of familiarity.

However, in what follows I shall be arguing that Heidegger does not succeed in bridging the gap between the ordinary and the skeptical attitudes. It will appear, as we go on, that Heidegger's final position is after all not that far removed from that of Descartes.

To bring out this point I shall first examine in more detail the relationship of *anxiety* to *fear*. These two moods are the two main forms of *Befindlichkeit* sustaining, respectively, the positions of the skeptic and the ordinary man. The presence of moods is crucial here for at least two reasons. First, the change from ordinary to total doubt is not brought about by any purely epistemic considerations but is due to a shift in the individual's attitude toward his own vulnerability. An individual defined by ordinary moods—an individual who feels himself vulnerable only in some specific areas and respects—can understand only ordinary doubts, that is, specific doubts raised for specific reasons. And so, the inquiry into the nature and kinds of doubt is part of a broader inquiry into the nature and kinds of human moods. Second, Heidegger's hope of bridging the gap between the ordinary and the skeptical attitudes is based upon his belief in the existence of a kinship between anxiety and fear. Because it is "anxiety which has been made ambiguous as fear" (*BT* 288), the thread of continuity between the skeptical attitude and the ordinary life is never entirely broken. This continuity is missing in Descartes, for the interests of the ordinary man examining and coping with ordinary doubts are totally different from the interests of the philosopher as he first entertains the hypothesis of the evil demon and then passes his judgment over the ordinary life as a whole. The continuity is not missing—or at least is not meant to be missing—in Heidegger, for the interest driving the ordinary man, the man who "perverts anxiety into cowardly fear" (*BT* 311), is to respond to the same human predicament that is also revealed in anxiety itself, that is, to our powerlessness and vulnerability in the world.

Now, the fearful attitude defines the entire issue of human vulnerability in terms of dependency upon persons, things, and goods. The threat is seen as coming always from a specific source within my environment and as calling for a specific and determinate response. Furthermore, not only is the source of the threat I am vulnerable to quite specific—an avalanche, a financial failure, a public criticism directed at me—but my vulnerability itself concerns only this or that aspect of my life: a specific relationship, project, or possession. Should I fail to realize that project or to hold onto that relationship, I can still go on with other endeavors; the defeat I have suffered is not total, for to begin with my vulnerability was not total. Of course, fear may also express my concern with self-preservation (*BT* 392). But what is important to notice is the way in which fear makes me define this concern: I refuse to face the fact that my life is at any moment (*BT* 302) at the mercy of death, and I attempt to forget and to weaken death's power over me by surrounding myself with persons, things, and goods.

In sharp contrast with such an "inauthentic" attitude toward death, an individual willing to accept the message of anxiety will live with an entirely different view of his vulnerability. His finitude will not be ambiguous any more, for he will courageously accept his mortality with all its "certainty" (*Gewissheit*) and "indefiniteness" (*Unbestimmtheit*).

Let us pay closer attention to these last two terms. They are the pivotal notions in an entire family of concepts meant to describe the very special status of death as death is revealed in anxiety. Without its certainty and indefiniteness, death would become manageable—at least to a significant degree—and so it would cease to impose upon Dasein the sense of utter powerlessness and vulnerability. Thus any attempt—as in fear—to gloss over death's certainty and indefiniteness is already a form of an escape strategy.

Death is "certain" in a much different—and indeed a much stronger—sense than either an inductive generalization or a proposition in a hypothetico-deductive system. Death's certainty is not that of an empirical generalization, for I do not need to go over some matters of fact to conclude—supporting my reasoning with the principle of the uniformity of nature—that I too must die. My death is known to me "a priori"; according to Heidegger, the sense of oneself as a mortal being is built into the overall structure of Dasein. Thus, whatever doubt one may want to cast upon the principle of induction, this doubt cannot erase one's sense of being handed over to the power of death. Similarly, at the very moment when the experience of anxiety makes me see the "artificial" and man-made character of the very principles of logic, I am brought face-to-face with my utter powerlessness to escape death. Now this certainty of the utter powerlessness can only be accounted for if the menace of death is also *indefinite*. To say that death's threat is indefinite is to say that it threatens me at every moment; it is to say that at no point of my life can I hope to build a wall against death. If the menace of death were not indefinite, then it would not have the kind of certainty that anxiety tells me it does have, for it would then be possible for me to dismiss the message of anxiety as not yet relevant to me; I could say, "I will still be around for a while," or "I don't have to worry about it yet"—and by saying all this I would already be interpreting death in the "inauthentic" categories of common sense: as a manageable event within the world, not as a radical threat to my entire being in the world.

We need still more terms to articulate death's total power over Dasein, and Heidegger does provide us with such terms in the course of his analysis. The evidence of death's power over us is so basic that "it does not belong at all to the graded order of the kinds of evidence" (*BT* 309); and the indefiniteness of death makes it a "constant" (*BT* 310) threat to us.

Let us contrast this immediately with what Heidegger says about fear. As we recall, fear is always a reaction to a specific threat within the world. This is why Heidegger is fully justified in putting forward the following statement: "If . . . that which is detrimental draws close and is close by, then it is threatening: it can reach us, *and yet it may not*" (*BT* 180; my italics). And again: "that in the face of which we fear is a detrimental entity within-the-world which comes from some definite region but is close by and is bringing itself close, *and yet might stay away*" (*BT* 230; my italics). But this also means that there is and there can be *no common measure* between what is disclosed in fear and what is disclosed in anxiety. For if I may be able to avoid or forestall the feared event, then one thing is clear: my certainty of the threat's power over me cannot be so unshakable as "not to belong at all to the graded order of the kinds of evidence." A specific threat from within the world—be it even this or that threat making me "fear for my life"—demands a specific response, and it always leaves room for my hope that it "might stay away." But such a description of the threat would be entirely meaningless if applied to death as death reveals itself to me in anxiety.

The implications of all this undercut the coherence of Heidegger's entire position on skepticism. In effect, if what I said so far corresponds to Heidegger's actual views, then the man of common sense would have perfectly sound reasons for dismissing the message of anxiety as utterly unintelligible. For if (1) the fearful, commonsensical man *can* successfully respond to a threat, and if (2) the threat itself *may not* materialize in the end, then (3) such a man can have nothing in common with the man who considers himself in principle totally powerless to diminish the margin of his vulnerability and who rejects any suggestion to the contrary as entirely meaningless. Any attempt at communication between the two men is now in principle impossible. Heidegger himself is driven to acknowledge as much when he says: "If with this phenomenon [anticipatory resoluteness] we have reached a way of Being of Dasein in which it brings itself to itself and face to face with itself, then this phenomenon must . . . remain *unintelligible to the everyday common-sense manner* in which Dasein has been interpreted by the 'they' " (*BT* 357; my italics).

Let us take a look at some further statements by Heidegger. Since in anxiety man realizes the precariousness of all his ordinary attachments—he realizes that death can take them away from him at any moment—a courageous attitude toward one's death "shatters all one's tenaciousness to whatever existence one has reached" (*BT* 308). Hence, "He who is resolute knows no fear" (*BT* 395). But the voice of the man who, against all evidence of common sense, believes that at any stage of our lives we are equally and totally vulnerable must sound like a voice of utter foolishness to the "inauthentic" man of common sense as he is described in *Being and Time*. His answer to the message of the anxious individual will be clear and well taken. Pushing aside the admonitions to face up to the "constant" and "gradeless" threat of death, the man of common sense will point to some irrefutable facts of life. Surely, he will say, I am *more* secure now, when I fixed my roof, than I was before, when the wood was all rotten. The tree may still fall over the roof? Very well then, I will cut down the tree. Won't I be more secure then? And what about all those other precautions I have taken: I have good health insurance, I drive carefully, I live in a safe neighborhood, etc. Isn't it obvious that my vulnerability has been dramatically reduced? His opponent, of course, may still refuse to concede. He may point out that no precautions and no defenses can protect us from, say, accidentally choking on a bone, or from being attacked by extraterrestrials, and so on. But, by now, the communication between the two men has—once again—broken down. The possibilities mentioned by the sceptic are entirely meaningless to the man of common sense. He will reply that such possibilities are only farfetched abstractions and not genuine live issues with which he should concern himself. If his opponent persists in questioning, the man of common sense will dismiss the entire skeptical discourse as senseless chatter. How could it be otherwise if in anxiety "what threatens is *nowhere*" (*BT* 231), while the man of common sense is concerned with avoiding threats which emerge with their own here and now? And how could it be otherwise if the threat seen in anxiety is "constant" and "not of a graded kind of evidence," while the threats disclosed in fear decrease or increase depending upon circumstances? To the skeptic, it makes no sense anymore to talk about grades or measures of human vulnerability. But this makes perfect sense to the man pursuing the paths of ordinary life; it is the speech of the skeptic that is entirely meaningless from the ordinary point of view.

So far we have only considered the *negative* function of anxiety: its awesome power to undercut the ties binding an individual to his public world. But, for Heidegger, anxiety has a *positive* function as well. While anxiety liberates man *from* his attachment to a form of life built upon a spurious search for security, it also frees him *for* a new commitment to a life of authenticity. Heidegger never loses sight of this second aspect of anxiety: "Anxiety brings Dasein face to face with its *Being-free for* . . . the authenticity of its being" (*BT* 232). Furthermore—and this point will now emerge as crucial to the present stage of our argument—while thus brought face-to-face with its freedom for authenticity, Dasein does not undergo a sudden metamorphosis into an isolated and free-floating self. On the contrary, Dasein now anchors itself firmly in the public world.[15] However, if this is to be the case, then at least some continuity ought to exist between the anxious Dasein and the men and manners of the ordinary world. But then it seems that our earlier analysis of the skeptical predicament must be deemed incomplete if not altogether unsatisfying. For if one's acceptance of the message of anxiety does not represent an insurmountable roadblock to one's ("authentic") activity within the public world, then the skeptical point of view cannot be altogether incommensurable with the viewpoint of the ordinary life.

There is, of course, one easy way of removing the entire difficulty. It is possible to misconstrue from the very beginning Heidegger's move by reading into it nothing more than some traditional skeptics' compromise with the *practical* requirements of living. For the traditional skeptic too does not intend to dwell permanently on the platform of doubt. At some point he will be perfectly willing, and indeed inclined, to abandon his skeptical detachment and to respond to the pressing tasks and needs of life by taking up the commonsensical attitude. He will simply deny to the latter any other—and stronger—claim to his allegiance. When asked about the nature of the hold the everyday world has over him, the skeptic will appeal vaguely to the necessity of survival and to all the beliefs such necessity entails: the belief in the existence of objects and persons around him, the belief in the veracity of his recollections, etc. But, the skeptic will continue, from the fact that we *must believe* in such things nothing can be inferred as to the *justification* of those beliefs; and thus the entire web of commonsensical beliefs will continue to be regarded by the skeptic as totally unfounded. If he, the skeptic, is willing to live within that illusory framework, it is not on account of its soundness and justification but because the skeptic *resigns* himself, after his meditation, to reenter the imperfect condition of ordinary mortals.

This is not, or at least ought not to be, Heidegger's position. While the traditional skeptic can proudly hold onto his identity—

actual or recalled—as a "philosopher" even while resigning himself to put on the clothes of ordinary mortals, the authentic Dasein has no such identity over and above its role in the public world. On the contrary, man's attempt to find an identity *outside* of the public realm is diagnosed by Heidegger as being only one more strategy of an inauthentic Dasein. A person dedicated to the exploration of his "inner self," allegedly buried, like a precious treasure, under the masks and facades of the everyday life, is in fact an alienated individual (*BT* 222), unable to organize his life in the public world into a meaningful pattern. In contrast, a truly authentic individual is described as finding his identity *within* the public world: "In resoluteness the issue for Dasein is its ownmost potentiality-for-Being, which, as something thrown, can project itself *only upon definite factical possibilities*. Resolution does not withdraw itself from 'actuality,' but discovers first what is factically possible; and it does so by seizing upon it in whatever is possible for it as its ownmost-potentiality-for-Being in the 'they' " (*BT* 346; my italics).

But while there can be no doubt as to Heidegger's *intention* of reestablishing the link—via his account of authenticity—between the anxious and the ordinary standpoints, it remains to be seen whether the overall conceptual framework of *Being and Time allows* for a successful carrying out of such an enterprise. Can anxiety fulfill its intended positive function once it has severed the link between an individual and his public world?

Put in this way, the question becomes even more important to the purposes of the present study. In effect, as I shall be arguing in detail in Chapter 2, Heidegger's theory of time is burdened by the very same difficulty I hinted at above when formulating my question. While Heidegger does not want to consider the ordinary, commonsensical view of time as an illusion, he cannot sustain that claim given his theory of the radical finitude of the temporality of Dasein. It will appear, once we take a more careful look at Heidegger's treatment of time, that man's anxious encounter with the radical finitude of his temporalizing makes it altogether *impossible* to take seriously the ordinary view of time as a chronological sequence. I shall now be arguing that a similar conceptual tension undercuts the coherence of Heidegger's ultimate account of doubt.

We must first spell out in what sense the authentic Dasein's identity is still bound up with the public world. "Resoluteness brings the self right into its current concernful Being-alongside what is ready-to-hand'' (*BT* 344). We shall take this statement of Heidegger's as our point of departure.

The expression "readiness-to-hand" (*Zuhandensein*) is meant to capture the status of items we encounter in our daily, practical commerce with the world. While Heidegger's description begins with what *might* look like the viewpoint of an individual self engaged in pursuit of his own goals, it soon becomes apparent that the entire intelligibility of the readiness-to-hand is shaped by a social context. Thus in order to occupy a position—any position—within the world of the ready-to-hand, Dasein must conform to public practices, norms, conventions, etc.

Let us start with a simple example of what Heidegger calls "equipment" (*Zeug*): here is the briefcase I use for carrying my lecture notes. The briefcase, we can notice immediately, is not related to me as an object I casually run across in my contemplation of the world. The briefcase is part and parcel of a broader context of my life; it has, in some as yet unspecified sense, a function in sustaining and making possible the entire sequence of my daily activities. The briefcase's immediate task—its "in-order-to," to use Heidegger's terminology—is to facilitate the carrying of my notes to the lecture hall. The lecture is the proximate goal—the "towards which"—of my use of the briefcase. Now all the proximate goals point toward a final goal which is no other than I myself: the lecture is delivered "for the sake of" allowing me to fulfill my role of a teacher. The briefcase, then, points to a broader "equipmental totality" (composed, in this case, of such items as the lecture notes, the lecture hall, the office where I receive the students, etc.) which in turn points to the kinds of goals and purposes I pursue. At every step of this system of references we can discover the ever-larger input of the public world.

First, a piece of equipment has a reference to the equipmental totality, and we cannot understand, let alone identify, the former independently of its place within the latter. The term "reference" (*Verwiesenheit*) has a special significance for Heidegger: it pins down the *constitutive* dependence of a piece of equipment upon its equipmental totality. The answer to the question "What is a briefcase?" will be unintelligible to someone totally unfamiliar with a way of life that includes universities, offices, or, in general, some institutions that depend upon individuals' ability to carry with them large quantities of paper. If one is not familiar with some such

general contexts, one will only be bewildered by finding oneself
confronted with a briefcase. This is why the readiness-to-hand is
not a *property* we can perceive on the briefcase considered as an
isolated object (*BT* 114). The relation with the office, the university, the loose sheets of paper, etc., is not indifferent to what it is
for this particular item to *be* a briefcase. Furthermore, those "referential" relations are still more special in that they cannot be for-
malized.[16] For the possible uses of a briefcase within our paper-
ridden culture cannot be spelled out in a *law* that some detached
observer could come to learn, thereby achieving the understanding
of what a briefcase is for. Thus neither an abundant body of information about the equipment's "properties," nor the knowledge of
"laws" allegedly governing the uses of such items, nor the combination of both could bring us any closer to the understanding of
the world of ready-to-hand.

How, then, *do* we understand and inhabit that world? It is at this
juncture that we can first grasp the rootedness of the world of
ready-to-hand—and hence also of the authentic Dasein, which is
meant to be a participant in that world—in our social practices.
"Dasein is for the sake of the 'they' in an everyday manner, and
the 'they' itself articulates the referential context of significance.
When entities are encountered, Dasein's world frees them for a
totality of involvements with which the 'they' is familiar, and within the limits which have been established with the 'they's' aver-
ageness" (*BT* 167). The statement is put forward after Heidegger
has analyzed, first, the structure of "significance" (*Bedeutsamkeit*)
and, second, the function of the "they" (*das Man*) as the general
and indeed the only depository of such a "significance." Were we
to envision an individual—be he inauthentic or authentic—as set
apart from the everyday world of the "they," we would be empty-
ing Dasein of any connection with significance. But since, as we
shall see in a moment, significance is indispensable to the securing
of *any* identity for Dasein as a being-in-the-world, the authentic
form of life must be seen as firmly bound up with the world of the
"they."

Already Heidegger's talk about reference has prepared him to
introduce the term "significance" into his vocabulary. For to say
that a briefcase refers to its equipmental totality—to the lecture
hall, to the office, etc.—is to say that the briefcase "signifies"
something to Dasein. *What* it signifies are its various referential

relations with other pieces of equipment: the briefcase is encountered *as* something to put the lecture notes in, something to be taken to the office, etc. "The relational totality of this signifying we call 'significance.' This is what makes up the structure of the world" (*BT* 120). We must talk here about the "world" for, in effect, a particular item cannot "signify" anything unless it is encountered within the appropriate environment: if that larger fabric of offices, universities, executive buildings, etc., were to be removed through some *Gedankenexperiment,* then the briefcase itself would stand out as an oddity. Now if significance is to be attributed ultimately to the larger fabric of the world, then the reason for Heidegger's move tying up significance with the "they" becomes easier to grasp. For the term "they" refers to the impersonal framework of social practices and norms through which the fabric of the world is first laid out and defined.

It can be objected at once that the "they," for Heidegger, carries only a *negative* connotation associated with Dasein's tendency to "fall" into the easy conformism of the average existence. Such are indeed Heidegger's best-known and most dramatic ways of characterizing the function of the "they." There is no need to review these descriptions here. But the function of the "they" is by no means reducible to that stifling and tranquilizing power of social conformism. The "they" is also the depository of significance, and in that capacity it supplies even the authentic Dasein with a sense of a world. "The 'they' is an existentiale" (*BT* 167)—that is, an all-pervasive way of being of Dasein—and "as a primordial phenomenon, it belongs to Dasein's positive constitution" (ibid.). Authentic life, therefore, can be seen only as a modification of the "they" (*BT* 168).

A further and more serious objection now can be addressed against the emphasis we have put upon the authentic Dasein's rootedness in the public world. For, it could now be claimed, even though all the world of the ready-to-hand is articulated by the norms and conventions of the "they," it nevertheless remains the case that an authentic individual could employ that world merely as a stage for the pursuit of *his own* goals and purposes. And those goals and purposes, one could claim, ought to be seen as set up independently of the "they" if we are to preserve any sense in which an authentic individual can still be viewed as not altogether lost in the anonymity of the public world.

Both the dispostion and the content of Heidegger's her-
meneutical investigation into the structure of Dasein in *Being and
Time* rule out the sort of interpretation we have just outlined. Immediately after offering his preliminary description of the everyday
world, Heidegger moves on to explore and to bring out the communal, social sources of Dasein's goals and purposes. This new step in
his investigation is implied by the steps already taken in the unfolding and deepening hermeneutics of Dasein. Heidegger first tells us
that Being-with (*Mitsein*) and Dasein-with (*Mitdasein*) are "equi-
primordial with Being-in-the-world" (*BT* 148), and he then goes on
to unveil the importance of these two items for the overall structure
of Dasein as a Being-in-the-world. Now if one focuses on the end
result of his analyses, one can see clearly that Dasein's goals and
purposes are *themselves* defined within the social network of the
"they." In contrast to the doctrine of Sartre's *Being and Nothingness,* where the goals and purposes defining an individual's
identity organize his environment around a unique "circuit of self-
ness," in Heidegger these goals and purposes are also elements of
the public world.

Let us return to our example. I put the papers in my briefcase
and I am on my way to give the lecture on the campus. The ultimate
"for-the-sake-of-which" of this system of references is my role of
a college professor. But this role *itself* is only a nodal point within a
larger network composed of other roles: those of students, admin-
istrators, taxpayers, and so on. In fulfilling the tasks associated
with being a teacher, I eo ipso acknowledge and take into account
all kinds of quite definite expectations, norms, and conventions
which keep me within the boundaries of a certain typical range of
behavior. I can, of course, be an "eccentric" or "atypical" college professor. But, first, in the overwhelming majority of cases,
such eccentricities are easily accommodated by the (relatively toler-
ant) environment of the contemporary academia. And, second, in
case my eccentricities overstep the boundaries defined by the norms
and conventions governing the behavior of college professors, my
status as an employee of the university will come to an abrupt end.
Even then I do not abandon the social world but rather move on to a
different slot within it (of say, a "dismissed" or "former" college
professor, on the lookout for a new form of employment, or devot-
ing his time to leisure, etc.). Whatever goals and purposes I do
choose at whatever stage of my life, they are all elements of the

social field of meaning in which I participate. The everyday world, therefore, is a with-world (*Mitwelt*) (*BT* 155), where all pieces of equipment and all equipmental totalities are used for the purposes that are *themselves* social through and through.

In talking about an individual "understanding" himself as a professor we are using the terminology Heidegger relies on to stress even more strongly the connection between the identity of any Dasein and the public world of the "they." In effect, understanding (*Verstehen*) is the *existentiale* underlying Dasein's capacity to choose itself: "The kind of Being which Dasein has, as potentiality-for-Being, lies existentially in understanding" (*BT* 183). But understanding is embedded in social practices and vocabularies. Hence in defining his own goals and purposes, an individual emerges inevitably as a social being. We shall now concentrate at some length on Heidegger's view of understanding, for it will appear, as we go on, that Heidegger's reliance upon the notion of the public, common understanding as the framework within which Dasein finds its identity is at odds with his theory of anxiety. And this is another way of saying that the gap between the sceptical and the ordinary points of view will have proven impossible to close not only for the ordinary, commonsensical Dasein but for the skeptic as well. Heidegger's admonitions to the contrary notwithstanding, the skeptic—educated by the message of anxiety—will find it altogether impossible to take seriously the public world of understanding and the roles laid out for him within that world.

Dasein's concern with and about its own identity is all tied up with Dasein's status as an entity "whose being is an issue for itself." It is not by chance that Heidegger returns to this phrase at the beginning of his treatment of understanding (*BT* 182). For Dasein "understands" insofar as it is—and must be—a "potentiality-for-Being" (*BT* 183), which is in turn grounded in Dasein's status as a creature whose being is an issue for itself. Man—to rephrase this last point—does not have a fixed and stable nature; his life is but a task to be defined and accomplished. In defining this task man takes a stand on what it means to be human by committing himself to a certain interpretation of himself and of the world. In his capacity to take such a stand and to define himself through such a commitment, man is "primarily a Being-possible" (*BT* 183)—a creature, that is, whose identity is not ready-made but *to be* made through his choice of different possibilities open to him. The possibilities of

Dasein, then, arise as live issues for it because Dasein itself is, in the last analysis, an unfinished, open-ended creature, a "Being-possible."

For this reason understanding—to which Heidegger attributes the function of defining Dasein's possibilities—must have the structure of "projection." In understanding himself, man, as it were, outlines himself and the path he will pursue in his life. Heidegger does not want his position to be confused with the theories of human person as a consciously thought-out life plan (*BT* 185), since any talk about such plans is too burdened with the intellectualist luggage Heidegger refuses to be saddled with. The outlined possibilities are not elements of a plan, for they are not posited in a free play of thought and imagination. In fact, quite the opposite is the case: since my projection first defines who I *am,* it limits in advance the range of possibilities I can subsequently inspect in my thought and imagination. And this point brings us to the issue that is central to our purposes in the present study. In effect, if projection is not to be confused with a free play of one's thought and imagination, it's because my possibility for being something or other is a "thrown possibility" (*BT* 183) where the thrownness of my Being-possible is precisely my rootedness in the public world as a pool of roles and identities to which I am confined in outlining myself in projection. For example, it is not possible for me, living in this day and age, to entertain seriously the idea of becoming a Roman legionnaire. This limitation of my options is not simply a matter of obvious physical constraints (there is no Roman legion around for me to join), for even prior to my thought of such constraints I will be struck by the oddity of the whole idea so much and so clearly out of step with the practices and the institutions sustaining our contemporary way of life. Conversely, the roles that are in any sense *real* possibilities open to the individual are all encountered—or at least delineated—within the social world of the individual. Such roles are "understood" by all of us, and their shared understanding is taken for granted as the background making up the substance of our lives. For this reason, understanding has the form of grasping something *as* this or that, and it indicates the presence of some form of meaning. Let us focus again on our earlier example. When I go through the motions of my daily activity, I conform to certain kinds of norms and conventions defining me as a professor. However deeply I may be immersed in my habitual daily routine, I will always have some notion of what that routine is all *about*. A sense of myself as a college professor gives a certain kind of regularity—if not outright predictability—to all my actions, beginning with the moment I get up in the morning and cast a nervous glance at my clock. Were I to lose that notion of myself as a professor, the patterns and the regularities of my life would immediately break down. To be sure, my conception of myself as a professor ought not to be confused with the Kantian *Begriff*. For, first, unlike the Kantian *Begriff* my notion of myself as a professor is not spelled out as a rule against which I will measure and organize my activities. And, second, such a notion *could* not be cast as a rule even if I were to make an attempt at doing this. Achieving understanding is, in effect, acquiring a *skill,* a form of know-how which allows me to master the role of a professor within our culture.

Since Dasein always understands itself, and since Dasein is a being-in-the-world, Dasein's world must also be understood in some way or another. This is why all items in our environment as we relate to them under typical circumstances are manipulated or perceived ''as'' something: ''to grasp something *free,* as it were of the 'as,' requires a certain readjustment. When we merely stare at something, our just-having-it-before-us lies before us *as a failure to understand it any more*. This grasping which is free of the 'as,' is a privation of the kind of seeing in which one *merely* understands'' (*BT* 190). Once again, the ''as'' is defined by the things' tasks and functions within the context of the public world. For the items I see as a clock, a briefcase, etc., derive their own meaning from their standing within all kinds of human pursuits (including my own) defined by the public world.

Naturally, I am not condemned to follow unthinkingly and unreflectively the routine ways of understanding a professor's role in society. I may attempt to reinterpret that role in order to gain a deeper sense of where I stand and what my life is all about. But, again, my interpretation is parasitic upon the very same forms of social understanding that I am trying to get clear about. In fact, interpretation emerges only as a possibility of and within understanding: ''The projecting of the understanding has its own possibility—that of developing itself [*sich auszubilden*]. This development of the understanding we call 'interpretation.' In it, the understanding appropriates understandingly that which is understood by it. In interpretation understanding does not become something dif-

ferent. It becomes itself'' (*BT* 188). And again: interpretation is
"the working out of possibilities projected in understanding" (*BT*
189). In effect, as Heidegger argues in detail, every interpretation
is *biased* and the interpretive biases (the "fore-having," the "fore-
sight," and the "fore-conception") are all conditioned by their
social context. And so the public world is always one step ahead of
me in that my own attempts to get a deeper and more original sense
of what it means to be a college professor are simply so many
different ways of expressing the strands of meaning deposited in the
public world.

But Heidegger also says: "Anxiety . . . takes away from Dasein the possibility of understanding itself as it falls, in terms of the
'world' *and the way things have been publicly interpreted*'' (*BT*
232; my italics). The difficulty raised by this statement is clear:
How can an authentic individual find his identity in the public
world *even while* remaining faithful to the message of anxiety?

Interpretation, we saw, is only a working out of possibilities
inherent in understanding itself. Now, every understanding has its
mood (*BT* 182). This means that man's grasp of the world as meaningful in some way or another is always dependent on the human
capacity to be *affected* by the way things are. If we could imagine a
creature totally oblivious to and emotionally detached from the
course of events, such a creature would not have any conception of
reality *as* this or that. The proposition applies, quite naturally, to
the average, common understanding.[17] Now, since interpretation is
based on understanding and since the understanding here at issue is
sustained by its own—ordinary and average—moods, any interpretation (no matter how original and deep) will not depart from
what can be understood within the ordinary moods. We remember,
however, that ordinary moods are only escape strategies used by a
Dasein unable to confront head-on the issue of its own finitude.
And so the ordinary understanding of the world is entirely built
upon an emotional stance of turning away from man's radical
powerlessness and vulnerability in the world.

For this reason alone, authentic Dasein would find it altogether
impossible to reestablish any bond with the mode of understanding
characteristic of ordinary men. To be sure, while the inauthentic
person cannot understand the authentic person, the latter can understand the former, since the temptation to "fall" into the reassuring
world of ordinary life is always an inviting option even for an indi-

vidual who has chosen to remain faithful to the experience of anxiety. But an individual who has chosen thus to live in the "unshakable joy" (*BT* 358) of authenticity will not be able to take seriously
the actions and the utterances of an individual paralyzed by "cowardly fear" (*BT* 311). For if moods are indeed the conditions of
understanding, then the understanding spawned by the inauthentic
Dasein will appear to an authentic individual as a *motivated cover-
up* of reality.[18] Such an individual will consider the entire everyday
world as a game to be suspicious of, and to hold oneself aloof from.

We have seen earlier how, given the standpoint of the everyday
life, the doubt imposed by the Heideggerian *Angst* appears just as
strained and unnatural as the doubt generated with the aid of the
evil demon hypothesis. We can now see how this similarity between Heidegger's and Descartes's positions on doubt extends to
the attitudes a consistent sceptic will have to take toward the everyday life, with all its epistemic certainties and commitments. For in
Descartes, too, the stance of doubt, when pursued to its ultimate
form, seals off the skeptic from the man of ordinary life. The famous problem of Cartesian Circle is only the main expression of
that state of affairs. Once the Cartesian self achieves the stance of
doubt, the vindication of the main body of human beliefs becomes
impossible without the divine stamp of approval bestowed upon our
clear and distinct ideas. But the proof of such a guarantee is
doomed to circularity: for unless the premises and the steps in our
reasoning are already secured by their grounding in God's guarantee, the proof itself cannot get off the ground. Either, then, the
skeptic will remain forever within the self-enclosed realm of total
doubt or, should he decide to break out of that realm, he will have
no choice but to fall back upon some beliefs accepted independently of his own standards. To put it still differently, either the total
doubt is not serious and consistent to begin with or, if it is serious
and consistent, the skeptic will never find any common ground with
the ordinary man. Both in Descartes and in Heidegger, then, the
skeptical position, when once asserted in its full radicality, cannot
lead us back to the beliefs of everyday life.

We shall now examine some further aspects of Heidegger's theory in order to gain additional support for our conclusion.

The self of an authentic Dasein shows a *constancy* (*BT* 369) that
is totally absent from the self of an inauthentic Dasein. To say this
does not mean to adopt the view of the authentic self as some en-

during mental *substance* preserving its identity throughout its changing states and experiences. But neither does it mean that the constancy of the self is posited as being merely—as in Kant—an empty *logical* form attached to all representations. There is no "bearer" behind our states and experiences; but, on the other hand, the unity of those states and experiences is secured not by an empty logical function of the "I think"[19] but by a concrete human agent taking a concrete, structured, stand on its own way of living. Insofar as man chooses the authentic way of life, his personality is not at the mercy of the changing trends and fads of the public world. His self is not dispersed into a series of disjointed stages and performances resulting from the individual's striving to find acceptance within the shifting conditions of the "they" world. An authentic individual will endow his life with a meaningful and consistent pattern which will run through all of his daily pursuits and endeavors.

Presumably, in order to be able to endow his life with such a coherent and meaningful pattern, an individual must be able to *give an account* of his actions. Clearly, a life composed of actions whose appearance and mutual relations would be unaccountable would not convey any sense of a common thread or continuity. An authentic individual, then, ought to be able to clarify and to make intelligible how the actions he is taking in the present are an extension of his past commitments, or how the actions he is envisioning for the future will be built upon the foundation of his present endeavors, and so on. Now man's ability to give such an account of himself—as indeed an account of anything—implies language. Language, in turn, is an inevitably *public* item. To the extent, then, that an authentic individual's way of life is to exhibit constancy and coherence, the individual must be an active and competent member of a linguistic community.

But, once again, it is not at all clear *how* an authentic individual could ever come to be a participant in such a linguistic community. For language, as we shall see in a moment, is also bound up with the everyday world of average understanding, while an authentic individual remains unable to take seriously that understanding *as a whole*.

It can be objected at once that the difficulty is not insurmountable, for it stems from our having blurred the distinction between discourse (*Rede*) and language (*Sprache*). While, it can be claimed, language is still—and only—a piece of *equipment,* which for this reason alone lends itself easily to the distortions of the everyday understanding, discourse must be seen as escaping such a predicament, since discourse is not an equipment at all but our most primordial way of disclosing the world. In that capacity, discourse would remain untainted by the superficialities and distortions of our properly linguistic communication.

Let us grant immediately one point to this line of criticism: in *Being and Time,* at least, language emerges as being built upon a prior—and nonlinguistic—way of disclosing the world. We remember Heidegger's earlier talk about "significance"—that in significance "there lurks the ontological condition which makes it possible for Dasein, as something which understands and interprets, to disclose such things as 'significations'; *upon these, in turn, is founded the being of words and language*" (*BT* 121; my italics). Significance, we recall, is attributed to the entire network of the referential relations within which particular items become meaningful to Dasein. These items are thus laden with "significations—they are encountered *as* this or that—and are therefore accessible to human attempts to *label* them with words. Language is the equipment with the aid of which Dasein captures and organizes the field of significance disclosed already on the level of discourse.

While one might find it difficult to accept the proposition that *any* significance could be given to man prior to and independently of its linguistic articulation, such is, indeed, Heidegger's emphatically stated position.[20] It is true that an experience which would be *in principle* beyond our powers of description and articulation could not become a durable possession of a community. But it does not follow, for Heidegger, that each and every experience appearing within the network of a shared understanding is necessarily linguistic.

Another point must be granted: language, for Heidegger, is particularly vulnerable to the power of social conformism. Heidegger's entire diagnosis (*BT* 266–267) of the traditional conception of truth is based on this assumption. For truth, when expressed and communicated in words—as it inevitably must be—becomes separated from the original place of its disclosure. It is now deposited in what is ready-to-hand—in sentences and paragraphs of a book, or in an oral report passed on from one speaker to another—and it is thus accessible to anyone, including the readers and the speakers who do not share the sense of that original disclosure. Their understanding of our written or spoken report may well be molded by the prevailing categories and clichés of the "they" world. And we will then find it possible, indeed inevitable, to wonder how it is that our descriptions can ever "correspond" to the things they are meant to capture. We will have ended up by considering the description and the world as two unrelated items.

But even though language, for Heidegger, carries with it the danger of such a drift toward the superficial and cliché-ridden ways of articulating the world, language is also necessary to sustain discourse itself. Language gives the latter the status of a durable, firm background of our shared understanding of ourselves. Hence no individual can escape the necessity of articulating his role within the language of his community. This is why, when Heidegger begins to analyze the functions of the "idle talk" (*Gerede*), he goes to great pains to emphasize the positive functions of the everyday language. On the one hand, language has a tendency to imprison Dasein within the bubble of catchwords and clichés that change constantly with the trends and fashions of the day. An individual succumbing to that form of language will lack any "genuine understanding" (*BT* 217) of that about which he is talking, writing, or reading. But on the other hand—and not surprisingly—public language has a positive function in that it conditions and makes possible any durable self-interpretation of Dasein: "The understanding which has thus already been 'deposited' in the way things have been expressed, pertains . . . to one's current understanding of Being and to whatever possibilities and horizons for fresh interpretation and conceptual Articulation may be available" (*BT* 211). Thus, if my identity is one of a college professor, I must conform to certain definite ways of describing myself and accounting for my actions. If, say, I am notoriously late for my classes, it is not possible for me to explain to the dean that I would rather watch my favorite soap opera, or go skiing before the afternoon crowd hits the slopes. Part of what is involved in my *being* a professor is that such ways of talking are not open to me at all. Should I use them, I would not be redescribing the role of a professor, but I would be giving expression to my disengagement from that role. To sum up: I cannot play any role in the world without depending upon a public and publicly available language.

Neither is it the case that Heidegger's distinction between language and discourse commits him to the belief in some form of a private significance. For while language does give permanence and durability to discourse, the latter is just as public as the former. In effect, discourse is always open to communication; but if discourse *can* be communicated, it's because it is from the very beginning shaped by a public understanding of our experiences (*BT* 205). More than that: the entire view of myself as a monadic, isolated ego endowed with some private experiences is only a deficient mode of a Dasein conditioned by the public world and identifiable within the public pool of self-interpretations (*BT* 155, 159).

But while the distinction between language and discourse is not essential to the line of investigation we are pursuing in the present study, the relation of both language and discourse to the point of view imposed upon Dasein by anxiety is highly relevant. Since both discourse and language are public, and since anxiety severs the link an individual entertains with his public world as a whole, an authentic Dasein will not be able to incorporate the stock of publicly shaped self-interpretations into *its own* perspective. If the public language is, as Heidegger claims, the depository of common understanding, and if that understanding, in turn, is totally sustained by the common moods—that is, by the moods in which Dasein turns away from its own vulnerability and powerlessness in the face of death—then the public ways of articulating and describing one's identity will have to appear, from the standpoint of anxiety, as so many ways of pursuing the ever-eluding mirage of security. To an anxious Dasein, the human need of conforming to the public stock of self-descriptions is simply an extension of the inauthentic Dasein's inability to endure a lonely encounter with death. An individual prepared to endure and to be lucid about such an encounter will have no reason to acknowledge and every reason to discard the public language as a whole.

Toward the end of Division Two of *Being and Time,* Heidegger undertakes a new attempt at demonstrating the authentic Dasein's ties with the public world. This new attempt is made possible by his conception of the *historicality* of Dasein. It turns out, as we make our way through the sections on historicality, that the authentic Dasein's suspicion of and toward the world of the "they" is balanced by a commitment to the *historical heritage* of Dasein's community. Even while suspending his allegiance to the world of the "they"—the world dominated by the ever-changing fads and fashions of the present day—an authentic individual rediscovers his historical roots and resolves himself to loyally follow his own heritage.

This project, needless to say, offers more promise and more hope than Heidegger's previous attempts at reestablishing the link between the anxious Dasein and its public world. To be sure, the latter now looks different from what it did to the man of common sense. For the man of common sense is all caught up within the ever-shifting trends of the "they." He has turned away from his historical roots in order to gain the security of fitting in with the expectations and values of the anonymous *Das Man*. But, at the same time, an individual who *forgoes* that security only *strengthens* his sense of belonging to a historical community. And this community, far from being an object of doubt and suspicion, is vindicated through the very same stance through which an individual tears himself away from the dispersal and the inconsistencies of the everyday world.

Can Heidegger make this move while still holding onto his own theory of anxiety? I believe he cannot, and I am going to argue this point by taking a close look at his treatment of the historicality of Dasein.

Heidegger's own formulations are quite revealing of the main—unchanged and unchanging—difficulty involved in his position: "Dasein's *inauthentic* historicality *lies in* that which—under the title of *'everydayness'*—we have looked upon, in the existential analytic of Dasein, as the horizon that is closest to us" (*BT* 428; my italics). The new terms in which we here confront the old dilemma are as follows. If the "everydayness" deploys the *in*authentic way of perceiving and living our historical past and if—as Heidegger argues at length in Division One of *Being and Time*—such items as understanding, discourse, interpretation, and language are all deployed on the basis of the ordinary, everyday form of human life, then a person's authentic access to the historical past would have to be achieved *independently* of any reliance upon those items. For if the public world and hence also the public understanding, language, etc., are all sustained by the inauthentic Dasein's motivated cover-up of the reality of human finitude, then the view of history achieved by and within that world must be looked upon with doubt and suspicion by an individual willing to live up in all lucidity to the finitude of his condition. *Either,* then, Heidegger has no right to confine the world of the "they" to (only) *in*authentic understanding of the historical past—but this is incompatible with his explicitly stated position as well as with the core of his own theory of the "they" world—*or* he cannot escape the conclusion that an individual resolving himself to live authentically will have to work out his *private* vision of the past, a vision, that is, unsupported by and severed from the practices and the vocabularies of that individual's public world. But this conclusion, although indeed inescapable in terms of the conceptual framework of *Being and Time,* is equally unacceptable to Heidegger, since it immediately invalidates his own stress on the inherently *public* character of an authentic Dasein's understanding and interpretation.

We can see at once the root of this dilemma: the *negative* and the *positive* functions of anxiety are at odds with each other and beyond any hope of reconciliation. Once the world of the "they" is diagnosed—due to anxiety's negative function—as the product of Dasein's flight from reality, the authentic individual will find it impossible to depend upon the public language and understanding in formulating his view of the past. But since, at the same time, there simply *is* no other source of language and understanding, the positive task of anxiety—the need of authentic Dasein to reaffirm its rootedness in the public world—cannot be fulfilled. In order to resolve this contradiction one would have to deny the very assumption that makes it inevitable: one would have to cease considering the everyday world as due to an entirely spurious attempt by man to erase and escape his own vulnerability. This is indeed the route we shall be taking in the Conclusion to the present essay. But this route is barred to Heidegger, given his entire theory of human finitude. Far from resolving the difficulty we have been focusing on all along, Heidegger's treatment of historicality makes the difficulty even more acute and more threatening to the coherence of his enterprise in *Being and Time.*

Two lines of investigation converge, in *Being and Time,* in leading up to the problem of Dasein's historical roots. To put it somewhat crudely, both the *form* and the *content* of authenticity imply the authentic Dasein's need to acknowledge and to live up to its historical past:

1. At its simplest level, resoluteness appears as an individual's way of assuming his fundamental *guilt* by taking up the responsibility for his life. But, Heidegger says (*BT* 353), to be truly resolute man must acknowledge the burden of shaping his life *as a whole,* that is, not just in this or that aspect and not just at this or that stage, but "right to its end" or "as long as it [Dasein] is" (ibid.). The end of Dasein, of course, is death. Hence resoluteness emerges as *anticipatory* resoluteness: "Only on the basis of Dasein's *whole* Being does anticipation make Being-guilty manifest . . . Only in anticipatory resoluteness is the potentiality-for-Being-guilty understood authentically and *wholly . . .*" (*BT* 354). Furthermore, man's lucid sense of his mortality leads him back to the sense of his birth. For—as we shall see in detail in Chapter 2—to say that man's temporality is finite means that man is a *determinate* creature. Now the determinateness of his life is due precisely to what he is *born into* (*this* particular family, culture, etc.). His birth, then, is just as much an inherent part of his life as is his death. And so in order to take a stand on his life as a whole, man must also take a stand on the situation into which he was born, that is, on his roots. The anticipatory resoluteness, therefore, must imply a commitment to give shape to one's life as it stretches from birth to death.

2. In opting for the life of authenticity, Dasein, as we saw so many times, is not meant to emerge as an other-worldly, free-floating self but as an active member of the public realm. The latter is what supplies Dasein with *any* identity—and hence also with the identity defining an authentic Dasein. Such an identity, Heidegger reminds us again, is to be found in the pool of possibilities into which Dasein is "thrown" by the contingency of its situation. But Heidegger also takes the new step we already have mentioned earlier. The possibilities that an authentic individual will take up and express in his life are not the current and superficial possibilities laid out by the "they" world; rather they are the deep, enduring values of Dasein's historical heritage.[21] This is where the anticipatory resoluteness finds its entire *content.* Moreover, it is not even *possible* to come to terms with one's historical heritage prior to and independently of one's ability to endure the finitude of human condition. As long as Dasein clings fearfully to the current world of the "they," it remains a plaything of the endless and endlessly changing fads and fashions of the day. Such a Dasein has a "plastic" personality, adaptable to anything and everything. In

contrast, a lucid sense of his mortality gives man an equally lucid sense of his thrownness (*BT* 438). As a limited and hence determinate self I cannot be "anything and everything": my identity is inevitably bound up with *these* particular roots that I have and that I cannot escape: "Only by anticipation of death is every accidental and 'provisional' possibility driven out. Only Being-free *for* death, gives Dasein its goal outright and pushes existence into its finitude. Once one has grasped the finitude of one's existence, it snatches one's back from the endless multiplicity of possibilities which offer themselves as closest to one—those of comfortableness, shirking and taking things lightly—and brings Dasein into the simplicity of its *fate* (*Schicksals*)" (*BT* 435).

An authentic individual's fate is inextricably woven with the destiny (*Geschick*) of an entire people. While committing myself to follow the path and to uphold the values rooted in my heritage I reestablish a link with the past of a historical community to which I belong. My acknowledgment of my fate amounts to a decision, on my part, of being *loyal* (*BT* 437) to that historical community—instead of opting for the comforting and ever-changing ways of the "they" world. Since fate is thus inseparable from one's loyalty to one's historical roots, and since the ways of the "they" world are incompatible with such a loyalty, an inauthentic Dasein can have no fate (*BT* 436). An inauthentic individual has traded off the sense of an enduring identity for the dispersed security of the "they" world. The bargaining strategy is still the same: an inauthentic individual is unwilling to accept his own historical roots, since doing so would imply his readiness to confront head-on the issue of human finitude. If I have a fate, then there are *limits* beyond which my life—both in its sheer span and in the values within which it can express itself—cannot extend. But an inauthentic individual is totally bent on covering up the limited and determinate character of the human self by pursuing the mirage of the endless possibilities of the "they" world. Such an individual, therefore, can have no choice but to deny his fate and to repudiate his heritage as so much dead weight to be left behind.

We are now in a better position to bring out the main difficulty involved in Heidegger's treatment of historicality. Let us state again this difficulty. *Either* the everyday world of the "they"—the source of language, understanding, etc.—cannot be interpreted as a sediment of the inauthentic Dasein's flight from the reality of

human finitude; *or*—and such is indeed Heidegger's clearly stated
position (*BT* 428)—since in fact only the *in*authentic view of the
historical past can be evolved within that world, the authentic individual's sense of his own historical past can be due only to a private, arbitrary insight achieved independently of the public
practices and vocabularies. But this conclusion is totally incompatible with everything Heidegger has been telling us about the inevitably *public* character of authentic Dasein.

"The authentic repetition of a possibility of existence that
has been—the possibility that Dasein may choose its hero—is
grounded existentially in anticipatory resoluteness" (*BT* 437). A
"hero," then, is a role model that an authentic individual finds in
his tradition and decides to emulate. But *who* are the possible heroes for me to choose from? Clearly, if my choice is to be guided by
some public standards, then I must fall back upon the pool of heroes selected in conformity with the practices and the vocabularies
of the everyday world. This world, we remember from Heidegger's
earlier analyses, deploys the only context of significance with
which I can be familiar. And so, in searching through my historical
past, I must focus on the figures considered "heroic" by the everyday world in which I live. But this world, Heidegger was telling us,
maintains an inauthentic vision of the historical past. The heroes of
that world—if there are any—are all selected to serve the latter's
changing fads and fashions: yesterday's heroes are quickly relegated to oblivion with the shifting trends of today. On the other
hand, were I to make an effort at finding my hero independently of
the "they" world, I would be falling immediately into the trap of
an isolated ego: the heroes that I choose would be only *my* heroes,
and my admiration for them would make me an oddity in terms of
the public language and understanding. And this is another way of
saying that the choice made by me would have been but a product
of my own fancy gone wild.

"Resoluteness constitutes the *loyalty* of existence to its own
self. As resoluteness which is ready for *anxiety,* this loyalty is at the
same time a possible way of revering the sole authority which a free
existent can have—of revering the repeatable possibilities of existence" (*BT* 443). As an authentic individual, then, I am to "re-
vere" an "authority." But who establishes for me that authority to
be revered? If the talk about a "revering . . . which a *free* existent
[my italics] can have" is to mean every authentic individual's right

to establish for himself what and who is to count as the authority to be revered—then authenticity implies one's private and arbitrary selection of one's own authority. "Freedom," on this interpretation, would mean freedom to choose independently of any available public standards guiding the choice. Clearly, this cannot be what Heidegger could have had in mind. But if the choice is to be made in conformity with our public language and understanding, then we are—once again—at the mercy of the changing trends and fads of the everyday world, since this world supplies us with the only language and understanding *we* have.

The life of a historical community is played out in its world. To the extent, then, that I regain the access to my community's past I achieve a different—and deeper—perception of my environment. The items that I encounter shed off their superficial and changing functions and stand out as endowed with a historical meaning. This building, for example, ceases to be a fancy restaurant, and it becomes once again one of the first buildings erected by the early settlers. "*With the existence of historical Being-in-the-world, what is ready-to-hand and what is present-at-hand have already, in every case, been incorporated into the history of the world.* Equipment and work—for instance, books—have their 'fates'; buildings and institutions have their history" (*BT* 440). But, as we remember, the ready-to-hand is laid out and organized within a context of significance deployed by the everyday Dasein. Conversely, anxiety renders the ready-to-hand, as well as the present-at-hand, completely meaningless (*BT* 231, 393). To an individual illuminated by the light of anxiety, the deeper historical layers of the ready-to-hand must appear just as alien as the present-day layers, since what counts as the *publicly recognized* historical significance of this or that item is dependent upon the everyday world, and it is thus caught up in the play of any trend or fashion of the day. But if an authentic individual undertakes *his own* attempt to dig out the historical significance of the ready-to-hand, he is, in effect, turning away from the public world and drifting toward the fictitious standpoint of an isolated monad.

The ultimate contradiction involved in Heidegger's position is not unlike the "hypocrisies" of subjective moralizing that Hegel has brought out and analyzed in the *Phenomenology of Mind* (*PhM* 615–641). On the one hand, we are told by the moralist that the *actual world* is the arena where the individual self must find its

realization as a moral agent. But, on the other hand, that world is
described in such a way as to be made totally unsuitable to the task
of embodying the striving of a self dedicated to a moral life of full
integrity and lucidity. And so the *actual* practices available in the
actual world must be regarded with extreme suspicion by the very
same individual who is called upon to realize himself in that world.
Unless, Hegel concludes, we are willing to vindicate the everyday
world, we will not be able to resolve the contradiction.

Faithful to this program of vindicating the everyday world,
Hegel takes an entirely different attitude on the more specific issue
of skepticism. The differences between the two philosophers' conceptions of doubt spring from the very same source as do their
differences on the issue of time—the subject we shall consider in
detail in our next chapter. In Hegel, the philosophical point of
view—the point of view adopted *after* the exploration of skeptical
experience—is entirely *continuous* with the everyday point of
view. Due to this fact the two points of view are open to dialogue
and understanding. But this also means that the scope of doubt is
much more restricted in Hegel than it is in Heidegger. The Hegelian
doubt is built *into* the epistemic commitments of the everyday life;
hence the philosopher can find sufficient reasons for hoping that the
ordinary man will eventually ascend to the philosophical standpoint. No such hope can be sustained in Heidegger. There are no
inherent contradictions and inconsistencies of the everyday life that
would induce the inauthentic humanity to enter the path of skepticism. This path, when entered upon by an individual, is opened
up for him by a sudden attack of anxiety coming from *outside* the
area of ordinary life. This is why, as we saw many times, the anxious and the ordinary standpoints are separated in the Heideggerian
account of doubt by an insurmountable wall. Hegel succeeds in
avoiding this outcome, but at the same time the Hegelian account of
doubt deprives this doubt of the depth that Heidegger is capable of
detecting in it.

The *standards of knowledge* are constantly at work and are never
suspended in the process of doubt as described by Hegel. When
Hegel sets out, in the *Introduction* to the *Phenomenology of Mind,*
to explore the road of doubt our prephilosophical, "natural" consciousness will have to travel on its path toward the standpoint of
philosophy he begins by noting that, as "knowledge of an object"
(*PhM* 141), consciousness has *within itself* the two components

needed to set off the process of doubt. On the one hand, consciousness is knowledge *of an object* set up as the "essence" or "inner nature" (*Ansich*) of things. Consciousness, that is, emerges from the very beginning as committed to some conception of a standard—of both reality and knowledge—against which our cognitions and beliefs will be assessed. The standard, let us add immediately, cannot be imposed from outside upon the prephilosophical consciousness, since Hegel's entire purpose is to show that such a consciousness, when employing *its own* standards and *its own* methods for testing them, will inevitably enter upon the path of the doubt leading up to the philosophical standpoint. This, Hegel thinks, is the only possible effective refutation of the natural consciousness's naive realism.

How *does* the examination of knowledge proceed? To the standard of knowledge and reality Hegel opposes knowledge itself: "In consciousness there is one element *for* another, or, in general, consciousness implicates the specific character of the moment of knowledge" (*PhM* 140). Not only do I have a standard of what counts as genuine knowledge of reality but, in addition, I have concrete cognitive experiences that correspond to that model. For example, at the stage of the standard posited by Sense-Certainty, the cognitive acts selected as pieces of genuine knowledge of reality will be the acts of simple sensing or intuiting: my mere seeing of a house, a tree, and so forth. But, moreover, natural consciousness has a need to examine the validity of its own standards. This need too is not imposed upon the prephilosophical consciousness by a philosophical observer: Hegel talks about consciousness's own "anxiety for the truth" and the "restlessness" (*PhM* 138) that will compel consciousness to test the justification of its own commitments and beliefs. Moved by that restlessness, consciousness will compare the "object" with the "knowledge" (i.e., with the effective cognitive experiences produced in conformity with our standard). In the process of this comparison it will turn out that our knowledge contradicts the object, that is, that our cognitions, when carefully examined, exhibit some features incompatible with the conception of knowledge supplied by consciousness's initial standard. For example, when examined in its claim to be a piece of genuine knowledge of reality, the mere seeing of a tree will have to articulate itself in language; but language, as universal, is incompatible with the standards of knowing initally set up by Sense-Certainty. Consequently, the examination of knowledge results in the repudiation of the very standard with which we began: "the standard for examining is altered when that, whose criterion this standard was to be, does not hold its ground in the course of examination; and the examination is not only examination of knowledge, but also of the criterion used in the process" (*PhM* 142).

But this also means that, for Hegel, doubt is always a *determinate* negation: we suspend a standard of knowledge on account of a *specific* failure of the standard, that is, for *specific* reason. The repudiation of our initial standard is, therefore, tantamount to the emergence of a new—and improved—form of knowledge (*PhM* 141). Doubt does not concern knowledge *as a whole,* and, what is even more important, we are told in vivid terms that from the perspective of *total* doubt no vindication of knowledge—of any knowledge—can be carried out.[22]

The Heideggerian anxiety, on the other hand, is meant to produce just that kind of doubt. While, in Hegel, doubt is entirely *continuous* with the ordinary epistemic commitments and beliefs, in Heidegger doubt suspends the entire framework within which such commitments and beliefs can be set up. The Heideggerian doubt concerns not the validity of this or that standard of knowledge but the very *concept* of such standards. For this reason, as we saw time and again, the Heideggerian doubt neither belongs to the ordinary epistemic attitude nor can it be evolved out of it. But while Heidegger—like Descartes—is capable of accounting for our withdrawal from that attitude as a whole, he is unable to establish any link between the ordinary and the skeptical standpoints. The view imposed upon Dasein by anxiety is entirely *discontinuous* with the commitments and beliefs of ordinary men engaged in ordinary pursuits. No dialogue can then take place between the skeptic and the man of common sense.

To get some form of such dialogue going we would have to meet at least one general condition. It would be necessary—and sufficient—to show that anxiety does not come from "nowhere" as far as the experiences of the ordinary man are concerned; anxiety would have to be shown to arise from the "inauthentic" moods sustaining the commonsensical attitude. In particular, a link would have to be established between anxiety and fear; we would have to show that fear cannot be seen as being merely one of the "illusions" (*BT* 311) of the ordinary life, a senseless strategy of escaping the inescapable. If the dialogue between the skeptical and the ordinary attitude is to take place, then the rechanneling of anxiety into fear must find some justification. It must *make sense* to the man gripped by anxiety to choose the path of fear in order to cope with the threat revealed by anxiety itself. Conversely, it must *make sense* to the man of fear to perceive anxiety as a possibility of his own life as he copes with the very specific and determinate threats in his immediate environment. Anxiety must map itself onto fear, fear must of itself pass into anxiety; the threat to the world must emerge from a threat within the world. Or, to put it still differently, the indefiniteness and certainty of death must be seen as being at least in some sense commensurable with the ordinary man's need for security. We must not distort and repress the message of anxiety, and yet we must find a way of vindicating the ordinary man's talk about "grades" and "measures" attributable to the certainty of death.

I would like to suggest that the puzzle can be solved. We shall be able to formulate the solution by taking a closer look at the violence of the struggle among men. We shall also discover, as we go on, that Descartes's evil demon is an important item in that solution. For Descartes's evil demon is a "demon" of a very peculiar sort. His features are merely the aggrandized features of *another man* as he is positioning himself to threaten my life and hence also my naive reliance upon the niche of the public world. The ultimate argument for skepticism—the argument unfolding the implications of human powerlessness and vulnerability—is indeed of a "demonological" nature, but the demon I am at the mercy of does not come from afar or from beyond, for he is a member of my own species.

TIME

Chapter 2

Perhaps one of the most striking features of contemporary philosophy is the importance attributed to the notion of human time. The significance of this notion extends far beyond the sort of interest a psychologist or a phenomenologist might have in investigating the temporal aspects of human life and thought. The importance of human time—"temporality" is the term used by many contemporary philosophers—shows itself again and again in such areas of inquiry as ontology or epistemology. In effect, once we are ready consistently to repudiate the notion of some fixed order of things, or the idea of unchanging epistemic standards, we are led to the notion of time—of human time—as to that which supplies the ultimate context of intelligibility and truth.

It is possible to argue that Hegel and Heidegger are the two most prominent representatives of this philosophical tendency. In their respective and equally famous phrases, "time is the existing concept (*Begriff*),"[1] "time is the horizon of all understanding of Being" (*BT* 39). But do the two philosophers really share the same theory of time? The question is serious, for there exists serious disagreements among serious authorities. For Alexandre Kojève, Hegel's great commentator, there is no doubt that the two theories are essentially identical. Both of them are built around the notion of *human finitude* (*ILH* 527), and Heidegger's *Being and Time* "adds nothing new to the anthropology of PhG [*The Phenomenology of Mind*]" (ibid.). Heidegger himself, however, is of an entirely different opinion. To him (*BT* 427, 428) Hegel must be seen as still operating with the traditional, "ordinary" notion of time first conceptualized by Aristotle and sustained by the attitudes and stances of an inauthentic Dasein pursuing its goal of making the world safe. To this tranquilizing notion of time Heidegger will oppose his own conception of human temporality as inherently limited by death and hence incompatible with any attempt to erase our powerlessness and radical insecurity in the world. In Kojève's view, however, Heidegger's claim to originality on this pivotal issue is entirely unsubstantiated (*ILH* 566). For as Kojève sees it, Hegel's theory of time is not at all meant to conceal man's limitation by death; Kojève will argue at length that for Hegel too a sense of death is indispensable to the emergence of our notion of time.

In what follows I shall be concentrating first on Heidegger and then on Hegel as interpreted by Kojève. Stated in this way, my purpose calls at once for some additional explanations and qualifications.

Let me note, to begin with, that it would be easy to refute Kojève's claim by simply adopting a different interpretation of Hegel.
In effect, if Hegel were to be seen—contrary to Kojève's entire
approach—not as a philosopher of human finitude but as a philosopher of the Absolute, then there would be no difficulty at all with
disposing of Kojève's more detailed claims concerning Hegel's
views on time. For then at some point the finite time would find its
grounding in the Absolute and thus time's finitude would have been
transcended and surpassed. But I shall not take this path for approaching the issues. The purposes I am pursuing in the present
study are defined entirely from within the perspective of human
finitude. Hence it will be much more fruitful to us to adopt the same
general approach to Hegel as Kojève did, and then to see, first, if
the Hegelian notion of time's finitude is indeed the same as its
Heideggerian counterpart, and, second, how both theories can
bring us closer to the core of the problematic of time as defined
from within the perspective of finitude.

Let me also explain why I have decided not to follow the historical order in discussing Hegel and Heidegger. The explanation is
simple: we will not be able to evaluate the soundness of Kojève's
and Heidegger's claims about Hegel unless we know beforehand
just what it is that Heidegger understands by the ''ordinary'' notion
of time, and how that notion is supposed to be evolved out of the
inauthentic humanity's search for security. Once we are clear about
these issues, we will be in a position to determine not only the
relationship of Heidegger to Hegel but, through it, the relationship
of time and finitude.

With these remarks in mind we can begin to examine Heidegger's account of time.

In ''anticipatory resoluteness''[2]—in one's courage and responsibility in the face of death—man expresses not this or that partial
commitment but his entire self as it exists between the temporal
boundaries of birth and death. For in anticipatory resoluteness man
lives up to the essential finitude of human time. This finite temporality is, in Heidegger's terminology, the meaning of Dasein's
being, that is, the meaning of care (*Sorge*). All items in the structure of Dasein, Heidegger argues throughout *Being and Time,* can

only be understood as aspects of care. But care, in turn, becomes fully intelligible only when we understand how Dasein "temporalizes" itself, either authentically or inauthentically. Since, in opting for the authentic way of temporalizing, man chooses courageously to live up to the *full* meaning of the finitude of his temporality, Heidegger begins his entire treatment of time by taking a quick glance at the overall structure of authentic temporality.

Now, the first thing that stands out in authentic temporality— and indeed in all other forms of human temporalizing—is the priority of the future (*BT* 378). Authentic temporality is disclosed through anticipatory resoluteness, and the expression "anticipatory" indicates the pivotal importance of my relationship to the future. Furthermore, only to the extent to which I envision and accept my future in all its finitude do I also envision and accept my past (and my present as well). To put it differently, man's authentic acknowledgment of his past (and present) depends upon his authentic acknowledgment of his future. Heidegger often insists on this point and supports it invariably (*BT* 373, 435) with the same argument. Once I accept death as my ultimate limit, my end, I am also led to acknowledge that I *am* a finite, limited creature. And so instead of losing myself in dreams about infinite possibilities allegedly open to me, I ought to try to make the best of whatever it is that defines me as a limited, determinate self. But what defines me as such a self is supplied precisely by my past—by my background, my personal history, my roots in a given collective tradition, and so on. I am thus led to *accept* my past. Similarly, my authentic stance toward the present is built upon my prior acceptance of the future and of the past: "In resoluteness, the present . . . gets held in the future and in having been" (*BT* 387). The road to the authentic present passes through the (authentic) future and past, for only insofar as I fully accept my limits—only insofar as I reconcile myself with the constraints of my past and the end of my future—am I capable of truly focusing upon the present, capable of being attentive and open to it. Conversely, when—in the inauthentic stance— I attempt to conceal and deny my finitude, my attention is all absorbed in a feverish pursuit of an ever-eluding security; I am thus unable to appreciate the present for what it is, I have no eyes and no ears for it, since everything I live by is elsewhere.

Heidegger's term for the authentic present is "the moment of vision" (*Augenblick*). In the moment of vision, then, I shake off all the artificial ties binding me to a mode of life predicated upon a spurious search for security and I become alert to and appreciative of my present experiences. I do not impose upon them some narrow utilitarian interpretation meant to serve my search for security. For the first time, I become open to things, I can finally encounter them for what they are (*BT* 388). I can thus separate what is truly important in a given situation from all the spurious values and functions projected upon it by my obsession with security.

This sense of accepting things for what they are can be found in the authentic past as well. The authentic stance toward my past is "repetition" (*Wiederholung*). We have noted earlier the dependence of the authentic past upon the authentic future. This dependence is the reason why, according to Heidegger, repetition is achieved only through anticipatory resoluteness (*BT* 437). In effect, once I accept myself as a mortal and therefore as a limited and determinate self, I declare the readiness to accept what makes up that determinateness of my self: my background, my personal history, the collective tradition of which that history is a part, etc. I am thus *loyal* to my past, instead of trying to deny it and escape it in order to adapt safely in the face of the ever-changing circumstances of life.

It will be of paramount importance to our future considerations to note at once that the future, the present, and the past as we have described them so far are *not* arranged in a chronological sequence. The anticipated future is not "after" the past and the present, and the repeated past is not "before" the present and the future (*BT* 375). Anticipatory resoluteness does not disclose death—the term of the future—as an event that "awaits" me at some chronologically further point of my life history. Death as my possibility is real to me in the very actuality of the present moment, for at every moment I am equally exposed to death's power. I am—or I should be—concerned about my finitude in every attitude I adopt and in every decision I make. Similarly, my past is not something that I have left behind, something that has simply elapsed and disappeared. My past is living in the present insofar as my background supplies me with that in terms of which certain choices appear as meaningful to me while others are felt as constraining and artificial. Finally (*BT* 387, 388), the moment of vision is not present, if by the term "present" we understand the position of an event in a (chronologically defined) "now." On the contrary, Heidegger's entire analysis of temporality is meant to show how the *chronologically* arranged sequence future-present-past is *derived* from the original form of temporaliżing where these three items are not at all chronologically ordered.

In contrast to the authentic temporality, the inauthentic temporality emerges from Dasein's strategy of refusing to face up to its own finitude. "Inauthentic temporality [is] . . . a looking-away from finitude" (*BT* 477). The issue of man's total vulnerability to death is now completely redefined. For an inauthentic individual, his vulnerability becomes partial and restricted to specific dangers which, the individual hopes, can be avoided and neutralized. This is what lies behind an inauthentic Dasein's frantic activity of building for itself a place within the reassuring niche of the public world. In addition, this activity itself soon becomes a source of tranquilizing, for it allows man to divert his attention away from the ever-present threat of death and to lose himself in the details and the trivialities of everyday life.

Once the focus of human vulnerability becomes shifted onto the stage of the everyday world of common sense, the entire meaning of past, present, and future undergoes a radical modification. All three of them are now defined by their function in the commonsensical, manipulative attitude through which the inauthentic Dasein attempts to conceal its finitude. To begin with (*BT* 386), the future takes up the form of "awaiting" and "expecting"—Dasein is completely absorbed in the pursuit of opportunities and in attempts to avoid misfortunes. An individual's entire identity is thus vested in his achievements in the everyday world of common sense. What those achievements are—what counts as failure and success—is defined by the impersonal power of "the they" (*BT* 386), incessantly secreting its pool of shifting images and "popular" roles.

Since our sense of the past is in general dependent upon our sense of the future, an inauthentic understanding of the future must entail a similar conception of the past. And, in effect, instead of loyally "repeating" his past, an inauthentic individual prefers to "forget" it. This forgetfulness of one's past reflects one's manipulative, commonsensical attitude toward the future. The inauthentic future is laid out in the form of a wide and indefinite range of shifting goals borrowed from the public world; in conformity with this vision of the future, the past is made into an object of a distorting, highly utilitarian attitude which constantly adapts the image of the past to the changing desires and expectations of an inauthentic Dasein. My past history, my roots, my tradition become all equally irrelevant now; what matters to me is a one-sided and ever-changing image of my past. For were I to be loyal to my past, I would have to make myself vulnerable to the blows of fate—an inauthentic, ever-quick-to-adapt Dasein can have no fate (*BT* 436)—and, ultimately, to that final blow of fate prepared for me by the power of death. But the strategy of common sense is to escape and to erase human vulnerability. By denying my past, by inventing a new identity for myself with every twist and turn of circumstances, I make myself into an ever-shifting target, and I thus succeed—for a while—in spilling over all the boundaries and all the limits. Like the Nietzschean slave, the man of common sense cannot be loyal to his past, for he simply cannot afford to be. All his past experiences are retained and remembered only on the basis of forgetting (*BT* 389), since his changing interests in the past keep alive only those slices of it, which are useful to him at a given stage of his life.

We have noted earlier the dependence of the authentic present upon the two other components of authentic temporality—the past and the future. We can quickly discover the same dependence in the structure of the inauthentic present (*BT* 376). In effect, one's manipulative, utilitarian posture toward the future and the past reduces all sense of the present to a "making-present" (*Gegenwärtigen*). Bent entirely on exploiting (future) opportunities and avoiding (future) misfortunes, an individual relies upon his established (past) skills and aptitudes in order to bring within his reach—to "make present"—a certain number of things and persons defining his identity. Furthermore, while originally such making-present is still targeted upon specific purposes, it soon becomes an end in its own right. This is where we can grasp it "most easily" (*BT* 397)—in that sheer "curiosity" (ibid.) which has freed the making-present from all connections with the pursuit of benefit or success. This is the form of making-present which "seeks to extricate itself from awaiting" (ibid.) and which drifts toward the extreme of a "merely making-present" (ibid.). Like Pascalian diversion, Heideggerian curiosity is meant to take us further and further away from the thought of our mortality.

Before we go any further we must clarify some important points we will need to keep in mind while examining Heidegger's overall view of temporality.

1. Although in temporality the ordering of the past, present, and future is not of a chronological nature, it does not represent a merely logical relation either. There is a sense in which our reference to the future must be made in (the not merely logical) terms of a "not yet," and, similarly, there is a sense in which our talk about the past would be meaningless without some notion of an "already." At the same time, these two expressions—the not yet and the already—must be kept free of any chronological interpretation such as "not yet now—but later" and "no longer now—but earlier." Considered merely as components of Dasein's temporality, the future, the past, and the present are ordered as pure "ecstases" (*BT* 347), as different ways of Dasein's being "outside-of-itself" (ibid.). Thus, in its attitude toward the future Dasein is (ecstatically) "ahead of itself" (*BT* 375), since the dimension of the future is opened up by man's sense of death as his ultimate and final destination. But that ultimate destination is not something man will have to worry about only "at a later date"—when he gets old, sick, and so on. As we remember, death's threat is of an "indefinite" nature, and it thus permeates all human attitudes and stances; it is an ever-present issue to man, a constant challenge he must meet and live with. The past too has an ecstatic character, for man's original conception of the past is all tied up with a sense of his roots, of his tradition, etc.; the past has thus the character of "already-being-in" a world (*BT* 375). But, again, it would be wrong to refer to the original past as to something that has merely elapsed and disappeared. The past is still alive, it is actual to me, for I can either deny or accept my roots and my tradition, but I can't lose them: everything I do is conditioned by where I am coming from and how I meet the challenge of coping with that. The challenge is with me constantly—Dasein "constantly *is* as having been" (*BT* 376)—and so too is the past. Finally, there is the corresponding ecstasis of the present: the "Being-alongside" entities encountered within the world (*BT* 375). We shall soon see how this ecstatical sense of the present, albeit irreducible to the chronological present, allows us to build a bridge with the latter. In effect, to say that man reaches out toward entities—to say that he preoccupies himself with rocks, trees, chairs, etc.—implies their *presence* to him, and this presence interprets itself as the *present tense*.

2. Temporality, we said, has an authentic and an inauthentic form. But this way of talking may still be misleading in the context

of an existential analytic of Dasein. For, as Heidegger puts it, temporality "is not, but it temporalizes itself . . . and it temporalizes possible ways of itself" (*BT* 377). This means that there are no forms or essences of temporality prior to and independently of the different human responses to the task of defining what it means to live as a finite creature. Let us take one example to illustrate Heidegger's point. There "is" an authentic form of the past only because man has devised a certain way of coping with his roots, with his "having been." It is not even legitimate to say that man "has" his roots—the way a plant does, for example—since what counts as his roots is always shaped by a stand he takes on them, by a commitment to a certain conception of what it *means* for a finite creature to have roots.

3. The conjunction of (1) and (2) allows us to assert two things: temporality is ordered nonchronologically, and it represents a form (the most fundamental one to be sure) of human activity. For, first, the order of ecstases—the future is understood as being "before" our present while the past is "already" behind us—is not a chronological order. "Temporalizing does not signify that ecstases come in a 'succession.' The future is *not later* than having been and having been is *not earlier* than the present" (*BT* 401). And, second, temporalizing is a form of human activity, since there "is" no temporality prior to and independently of human responses to the task of defining what it means to be a finite, mortal creature.

4. From this second point made under (3), it follows immediately that the commonsensical belief in the alleged "objectivity" of time is an illusion of an inauthentic Dasein which "does *not* know this 'time' as its own" (*BT* 464). In order to discover the man-made character of time as ordinarily understood, one would have to be able to unmask the strategy responsible for its emergence. But in order to be able to unmask that strategy, one would first have to come to terms with one's inherent finitude. Only anxiety can lead an individual onto that path, but anxiety spells the collapse of the commonsensical world as a whole.

But—we shall now have to ask Heidegger—what *does* happen to our sense of time when anxiety reveals to Dasein the artificial and man-made character of time as ordinarily understood? Let us be more precise. If anxiety brings me face-to-face with the inherent finitude of my temporalizing and if, from this (philosophical) point of view, time as ordinarily understood turns out to be a deposit of

Dasein's *entirely spurious* search for security, is it still possible to establish a link between the philosophical and the ordinary notions of time?

In order to decide this issue we must first pay closer attention to the steps through which Heidegger derives time as ordinarily understood from the finite temporality of Dasein. The derivation takes off with the discovery of the *horizonal schemata* of temporality.

The three temporal ecstases are not, originally, arranged in a chronological order. However, we soon discover that each of these ecstases defines itself by a horizonal schema due to which it is projected onto the world. As a result, two things happen: *(a)* temporality is mapped onto the world in the form of world-time, and *(b)* entities are arranged within a temporal chronology.

Let us note at once the striking similarities between Heidegger's present move and Kant's theory of schematism. These similarities are attested to not only by the subject matter itself but by the very terminology Heidegger employs—it is not by chance, after all, that he talks about the "schemata" of temporality—as well as by the main line of his interest in Kant in *Kant and the Problem of Metaphysics*. For Kant, the problem of schematism arises within the context of his attempt to account for the application of pure categories to sensible manifold. In effect, since the pure categories spring from understanding while the pure manifold is supplied by sensibility, it is not at all clear how the former can be made applicable to the latter. Kant's solution is to appeal to the schematism of pure categories. The schemata are meant to supply the missing link between the pure categories on the one hand and the data of the senses on the other hand. In a similar vein, the Heideggerian schemata of the three temporal ecstases allow us to establish the connection between the original temporality of Dasein and the chronological sequence of the ordinary time.[3]

In each of the three horizonal schemata the "horizon" is different and so the corresponding ecstasis is differently projected onto the world. Let us take, as the first example, the horizonal schema of the past. This schema is defined as "that *in the face of which* [Dasein] has been and that to which it has been abandoned" (*BT* 416). Man, we have noted earlier, has a past insofar as he is a determinate self, enclosed within the boundaries of his roots, his background, etc. To the extent to which man finds himself defined by such and similar conditions, all of his activities are conditioned

activities: they take place within a given and inherited state of social customs, practices, technologies, etc.; briefly, within a certain
state of the world. This state of the world is the springboard for all
human endeavors and, in that capacity, it is always found as "that
in the face of which" each individual finds himself while defining
and implementing his goals. In other words, when I think of my
past—when I think of where I am coming from—I think of the
conditions I found around me and had to take into account while
establishing and pursuing my goals. And this reference of my past
to the conditions of my actions is precisely the schema of the ecstasis of the past. Due to this schema the sense of my past is
mapped onto the world: I think of my own "having been" in terms
of what I have found around me, that is, in terms of the world. My
past is thus reflected in the past of the world; a pure ecstasis of
temporality receives its world horizon. All items of the world can
then be ordered and arranged within that horizon. This final
move—we will come back to it in a moment—is, again, identical
with the solution ultimately adopted by Kant. Just as the kinship of
the Kantian schemata with the *pure* form of sensibility makes it
possible to account for the application of the categories to the *empirical* data of the senses, so too the schematization of ecstases onto
the world secures the subsumption of entities—of trees, houses,
etc.—under the ordinary temporal framework ("world-time," as
Heidegger calls it).

I have started out by discussing the horizonal schema of the past,
but it is especially the corresponding schema of the present that is
of crucial importance to Heidegger's theory of time and indeed to
his fundamental ontology as a whole. For the schema of the ecstasis
of the present is "praesens" (*BPP* 306), where "praesens" is
nothing less than the pivotal paradigm underlying the entire "metaphysics of presence"—our own Western metaphysics—which it is
Heidegger's ambition to overcome.

Things of use—implements, pieces of equipment, forces of
nature harnessed for the benefit of man, etc.—are shaped and
formed by Dasein's productive activity and set up in the world as
"something established stably for itself" (*BPP* 108). The house,
the trees, the car in the garage are all deployed around us in their
status of enduring and disposable items we rely upon in pursuit of
our purposes. They are—as we noted earlier—"present" to us in
that very elementary sense of being always there for us when we

need them, thanks to their endurance independently of momentary acts of attention or distraction on our part. Their being, then, has a "praesensial meaning" (*BPP* 305) to us, it is "praesens" (*BPP* 306). But the presence here at issue ought not to be confused with the (chronologically determined) present *tense,* that is, with the "now." Praesens is more original than the now, and, further, it constitutes the condition of possibility of the latter. Producing things and setting them up as disposable items is called "enpresenting"[4] them. Enpresenting, in turn, is a mode of temporalizing: "Enpresenting is the ecstasis in the temporalizing of temporality which understands itself as such open upon praesens. As removal to . . . , the present is a being-open for *entities confronting us,* which are thus *understood antecedently upon praesens*" (*BPP* 306–307). Furthermore—we shall soon explain this point in more detail—the chronologically situated "now" will arise out of the interpretation of "praesens" in terms of the items with which man is preoccupied in his daily living.

The items stamped with a "praesensial meaning"—the items set around Dasein as enduring, reliable entities—are the paradigms around which the metaphysics of presence builds its model of reality. The Aristotelian ousia, being, actuality, existing are all conceived as such enduring enpresented items (*BPP* 109). Our traditional conceptions of a thing's "essence" also spring from that source. To have something present-at-hand is to know "what" it is that one has thus produced and set up in the world as an enduring entity. In producing and surrounding himself with things man beholds the eidos or the essence of things (ibid.). The concepts of existence and of essence, then, acquire their meaning from the horizonal schema of the ecstasis of the present. Since, in addition, producing and surrounding oneself with things is for the most part due to the *in*authentic Dasein's search for security in life and thought, the "enpresented" items are posited—both in their existences and in their essences—as entirely independent of Dasein itself. Only thus can the activities of (inauthentic) Dasein receive the desired firm grounding in the order of things.

The move from the ecstasis to its schema is only the first step in Heidegger's derivation of time as ordinarily understood. The next step is announced at the beginning of the last chapter of *Being and Time,* and it is then systematically developed throughout that chapter. We have already hinted, in general terms, that due to the sche-

matization of ecstases all pieces of the world's furniture are
arranged within "world-time." But we do not yet know how this
within-timeness (*Innerzeitigkeit*) of entities amounts to the
emergence of the ordinary chronology as we encounter it in our
daily practice of "reckoning with time" or "taking time into account." It is to this task that Heidegger now turns.

When I refer to the time of something—of an action, of a process, of an event—I "assign time to it" (*BT* 461); I say this or that
will take place "then," it will endure that long, etc. Now, since
this practice of reckoning with time first emerges within the commonsensical attitude and since that attitude as a whole is due to the
inauthentic Dasein's search for security, we will not be surprised to
learn that the inauthentic temporality is at the origin of the practice
of reckoning with time. In effect, as Heidegger argues at length (*BT*
458–461), inauthentic temporality—and especially inauthentic
present—is what first moves Dasein to "assign time" to entities.
We need only take a closer look at the inauthentic present—at the
stance of "making-present" Heidegger has been expounding on at
the earlier stages of his argument in *Being and Time*. We soon
notice that the making-present "interprets" itself in terms of the
entity to which it "addresses" itself. Let us convey Heidegger's
point with the aid of an example. When I bring something within
my reach—when, for example, I bring my new car to my garage—
I establish it as durably disposable, as "present" to me. Since the
presence of the thing is thus the result of my own making-present,
and since the stance of making-present is temporal, the thing's
presence is interpreted as the present *tense*. This is why the presence of things to me is expressed by my talk of them as given to me
"now" or "at the present moment." Of course, something can be
absent at the present moment: a book may be missing from the
shelf, my hammer may not be in the toolbox, etc. But, as Heidegger points out elsewhere (*BT* 406; *BPP* 305), such missing is in fact
a deficient mode of presence: by looking over the shelf and the
toolbox I feel the actual absence of the book and of the hammer; the
shelf and the box "look empty," as it were, and this emptiness is
the present trace of the missing items.

The inauthentic present is inseparable from the inauthentic past
and future, and so the interpretation of making-present entails the
corresponding interpretation of awaiting and retaining: "The making present which awaits and retains interprets *itself*" (*BT* 460).

The interpretation of awaiting yields the chronologically situated "then" (in the sense of "by then, I shall be ready to do this or that," etc.), while the retaining is expressed through reference to what happened "on that former occasion." This is how the original ecstases of the past and of the future are redefined as being, respectively, something "earlier" and something "later" than the present.

The temporal chronology we have now derived is firmly bound up with the inauthentic Dasein's absorption in the work world. Thus, for example, when we assign *dates* through the expressions "now," "earlier," and "later" we refer originally to some object of our practical concern. "Now" means originally "now *that* so and so is happening," "now *that* I am finally ready to do so and so," etc. Similarly, the "span" of time—the enduring or lasting of a determinate temporal period—first emerges from our practical concern with entities. If I await a return on my financial investments in order to buy a house, I know that I will not be in a position to have a house *until* my investments pay off. I must postpone my desire "until then," and this is how I first gain a conception of temporal enduring. When I say that I reckon with time or that I take time into account, I mean first of all time as I measure it by the arrangement of entities and tasks encountered within the work world.

Heidegger then proceeds to demonstrate how the purely theoretical notion of time as a homogeneous series of "nows" is derived through the leveling off of the time of the work world. We need not concern ourselves with this further demonstration. Once the notion of a temporal chronology is established—be it even the notion of chronology encountered in the work world—it then becomes possible to trace its further forms and specifications. Our question is more fundamental. *Is* it possible to derive the notion of a temporal chronology—of *any* temporal chronology—from the finite temporality of Dasein? To this question we must now turn.

Our critical examination of Heidegger's positions will follow the pattern we have adopted in Chapter 1. As we saw in that chapter, Heidegger could establish no link between an individual's clear sense of his own finitude and his commitment to the practices and the vocabularies sustaining the ordinary world. The existence of such a link was required by Heidegger's entire account of skepticism, but, as we saw, the conceptual framework of *Being and*

Time would not *allow* us to meet this requirement. We shall now argue that Heidegger's theory of time fails for a very similar reason.

The theory's main purpose is, again, to do justice to two distinct and equally important claims. On the one hand, time as ordinarily understood is meant to be derived as a "genuine phenomenon" (*BT* 374, 382) and not a mere illusion. This is why an authentic individual, that is, an individual living with a clear sense of finite temporality disclosed in anxiety, is not to be construed as some sort of an otherworldly self but as an active participant in the ordinary world and hence also as seriously taking time into account in his daily practices of "reckoning" with time. But, on the other hand, Dasein's coming face-to-face with the ultimate meaning of its Being— with finite temporality—demolishes the entire significance of the ordinary world and hence also the significance of commonsensical time. I shall now be arguing that these two components of Heidegger's theory—(1) time as viewed by common sense is derived from finite temporality, but it is derived as a genuine phenomenon, not as a mere illusion; and (2) an individual lucidly aware of finite temporality can attribute no meaning at all to time as viewed by common sense—are totally incompatible.

Once again, the difference between *fear* and *anxiety* will lead us onto the main difficulty involved in Heidegger's position. In effect, the "authentic" grasp of temporality is shaped by, among other things, Dasein's willingness to accept and to live with the message of anxiety, while the option for a form of life restricted to the commonsensical notion of time is built upon fear, since fear, as we recall from Chapter 1, is the main mood underlying the commonsensical attitude as a whole, and hence also the commonsensical view of time. This role of fear and anxiety is made clear by Heidegger himself in his explicit discussion of the specifically *temporal* aspects of the difference between fear and anxiety. It is no accident that this discussion takes place in the chapters on time; in effect, Heidegger's entire treatment of the problematic of time would become incomprehensible without a clear conception of what fear and—particularly—anxiety reveal to us about the status of temporality.

Since fear is at the root of the commonsensical attitude as such, the temporality of fear exhibits all the salient features of inauthentic temporality. This means, first of all, that the inescapable finitude of

Dasein's temporality is not being faced up to but is concealed and covered up. The issue of Dasein's mortality is redefined in terms of the everyday world; death loses all its certainty and indefiniteness and it becomes bound up with specific dangers encountered within the world, dangers which are open to human management and control. In fear, the human concern over death translates itself into concern about "self-preservation and evasion" (*BT* 392). Hence an individual becomes dedicated to avoiding everything that may endanger his life and searching for everything that may offer him additional security. The search for a risk-free existence is rechanneled into the tunnel of the inauthentic future as man fearfully awaits what is in store for him. This "fear of the morrow" is, at the same time, the cause of the inauthentic Dasein's *forgetting* of its own past. For, as we saw earlier, an inauthentic individual's conception of his past is mutilated by the ever-changing ways of adapting safely to the circumstances of life; an inauthentic individual retains from his past only what can serve him in his search for security and he relegates everything else to oblivion. Finally (ibid.) fear conforms to the logic of the inauthentic present: fear is an obsessive "making-present" bent on bringing within one's reach an indefinite number of items (a house, a health insurance, a retirement plan, etc.) meant to guarantee security and to divert one's attention from the inescapable menace of death.

Once inauthentic temporality is laid out in one's fearful search for security, the emergence of temporal chronology is a matter of course. In effect, inauthentic temporality—the temporality of a Dasein fearfully absorbed in the world—"interprets" itself in terms of items to which inauthentic Dasein clings in its search for security. Thus, as we already saw, making-present interprets itself as the presence of things in a "now"; awaiting interprets itself through its reference to what will come "later"; while the inauthentic past is mapped onto the world as an "earlier."

Let us quickly mention—and remove—an apparent confusion in Heidegger's account. While Heidegger's main move is to derive time as ordinarily understood from *in*authentic temporality, he also seems to be saying that the ecstases of both the inauthentic *and* the authentic forms of temporality "interpret" themselves in chronological terms. This is what is clearly implied by Heidegger's theory of horizonal schemata. The schemata are to be found in *both* forms of temporality—for example, Heidegger talks about "the schema in which Dasein comes towards itself *futurally,* whether authentically or inauthentically'' (*BT* 416)—and since the schemata are instrumental in mapping temporality onto the world, it is clear that authentic temporality too must include a reference to the chronologically ordered time of the world.

But there is no confusion here. Authentic temporality is firmly bound up with the time of the world—and hence also with all the more sophisticated practices of ''reckoning with time'' through the use of natural and artificial *clocks*—for the very simple and entirely sufficient reason that authentic Dasein is not a free-floating, otherworldly self but an individual living in the ordinary world. In Heidegger's words: ''Authentic Being-one's-Self does not rest upon an exceptional condition of the subject, a condition that has been detached from the ''they''; *it is rather an existentiell modification of the ''they''—of the ''they'' as an essential existentiale''* (*BT* 168). The proposition is quite general, and it applies to authentic temporality as well. An individual who courageously lives up to the inescapable finitude of temporality is meant to be an active participant in the ordinary world, which is defined by some form of temporal chronology; hence the ecstases of authentic temporality must be conformable to a chronological interpretation. But, on the other hand, the connection of *in*authentic temporality with the time of the ordinary world is more direct, since that world itself first emerged from an inauthentic Dasein's single-minded pursuit of security.

To the temporality of fear Heidegger opposes the temporality disclosed in anxiety (*BT* 393–395). Now, although the sense of temporality disclosed in anxiety must be preserved in authentic temporality, the temporality of anxiety and the authentic temporality are by no means identical. Anxiety imposes a view of temporality to which an individual can *then* respond either authentically or inauthentically, that is, by deploying either the authentic or inauthentic form of temporality. Thus the (purely) anxious conception of the past, the present, and the future is different from both their authentic and their inauthentic forms. While both the authentic and the inauthentic temporality are connected—although in different ways—with the time of common sense, the temporality of anxiety spells the collapse of the commonsensical notion of time. It then becomes possible—and indeed necessary—to inquire whether the commonsensical notion of time, when once suspended by anxiety, can ever again be taken seriously by Dasein. And this is the main question we set out to ask in connection with Heidegger's theory of time as a whole.

Let us pay closer attention to the temporality of anxiety. Heidegger goes to great pains to bring out the difference between the *present of anxiety* on the one hand and both the authentic and the inauthentic present on the other hand.

"In contrast to this [inauthentic] making-present which is not held on to, the Present of anxiety is *held on to* . . . but even though the Present of anxiety is *held on to,* it does not as yet have the character of the moment of vision [of the authentic present] which temporalizes itself in a resolution" (*BT* 394).

Similarly, the *past of anxiety* is altogether different from both the inauthentic and the authentic past:

"This bringing-back has neither the character of an evasive forgetting nor that of a remembering [of the inauthentic past]. But just as little does anxiety imply that one has already taken over one's existence into one's resolution and done so by a repeating [as in the authentic past]" (ibid.).

These statements fit in very well with Heidegger's entire theory; in fact, they are implied by it. For if anxiety "discloses the insignificance of the world" (*BT* 303)—if, that is, anxiety alienates an individual from the ordinary world of public practices—then the view of time disclosed by anxiety will have no connection whatever with time as ordinarily understood.

This is also why the temporality of anxiety will differ even from authentic temporality. All of this is implied by Heidegger's theory and all of this is clearly stated in the passages we have just quoted.

Since anxiety grips us in the face of death, and since, further, the ordinary view of time is altogether suspended by anxiety, it follows that the threat of death as disclosed by anxiety cannot be localized within any kind of temporal chronology. This is a straightforward inference from Heidegger's position, and it is, again, perfectly consistent with the latter. The indefiniteness of death—death can strike us "at any moment"—ought not to be construed (terminological difficulties notwithstanding) in any chronological sense. The ever-present threat of death cannot be *dated*—the expression "at any moment" ought not to be in-

terpreted as meaning "in any now"—since the sense of such a
threat (fled from or faced up to) is the very condition of there being
any dates at all.

But if the talk about the indefiniteness of death is not to be given
the ordinary chronological interpretation, and if the latter is altogether suspended by anxiety, then the situation turns out to be
exactly the same as the one we have already confronted while examining Heidegger's position on skepticism. Once again, the ordinary and the philosophical (the anxious) standpoints emerge as
separated by an unbridgeable gap. The man of ordinary life can
have no understanding of or use for the anxious conception of time,
while the man viewing time from the vantage point of anxiety must
consider the ordinary conception of time as entirely illusory. Once
again, the ordinary man will stubbornly hold that death is *less* certain in some "nows" ("now, that I have a good health insurance
policy," "now, that I live in a safe neighborhood," etc.) than it
was in other "nows"; hence it follows at once that the threat of
death *can* be described by reference to our ordinary chronology of
events. And, once again, the man seized by death's apocalyptic
("indefinite") threat to him will stick to his belief that the end of
the world is always equally a possibility.

Were we to be able to attribute some meaning to the ordinary
view of time *even while* adopting the vantage point of anxiety, we
would have to show that death's indefinite threat to man is open to
some form of the ordinary, chronological interpretation. In other
words, we would have to show that even in—and in spite of—
anxiety, the temporal ecstases are conformable to an interpretation
onto the ordinary world. But this is incompatible with Heidegger's
overall philosophical position and, more important, it is incompatible with his theory of temporality.

This is why the temporality of anxiety has no *horizontal schemata.* No mention of them is to be found in *Being and Time,* and,
of course, Heidegger is prefectly consistent in this refusal to attach
schemata to the ecstases of anxious temporality. For the schemata
are meant to produce the interpretation of the ecstases in terms of
the ordinary world; where no such interpretation can take place, no
schemata are to be found. In fact—and to put our point in even
stronger terms--it is difficult to avoid the conclusion that the entire
schematization of ecstases is either impossible or unnecessary. If
we begin with the forms of temporalizing defined by man's active

participation in the ordinary world, then the schematization of ecstases is unnecessary, for those ecstases are already mapped onto
the world: it makes no sense to talk about an ecstasis "prior to" its
schematization, since the forms of temporalizing here at issue cannot be separated from their interpretations in terms of the world. On
the other hand, were we to sever the connection between temporality and the ordinary world—were we to consider finite temporality from the vantage point of anxiety—we would be in no
position to show how temporality interprets itself in terms of the
world. No schematization would help us at this point, since all links
between the temporal ecstases and time as ordinarily understood
would have been destroyed by anxiety.

To sum up: when (anxiously) discovered in all its finitude,
human temporality turns out to be totally alien to man's ordinary,
everyday experience of time. No bridge can then be built between
these two notions of time.

However, some of Heidegger's formulations in *Basic Problems
of Phenomenology* raise at least one difficulty for our conclusion.
The difficulty is implicit in Heidegger's detailed theory of the relationship between the two key aspects of human temporality: temporality as *Zeitlichkeit* (in English translation: temporality) and
temporality as *Temporalität* (in translation: Temporality). For if it
can be claimed that anxiety cannot set *Zeitlichkeit* apart from *Temporalität*, then the original doctrine of the temporality of anxiety
(and indeed Heidegger's entire teaching on anxiety) will have to be
repudiated.

The distinction between *Zeitlichkeit* and *Temporalität* is introduced in order to account for two different functions of human
temporalizing. As *Zeitlichkeit*, temporality is taken to be the condition of the possibility of *Dasein itself* (*BPP* 274). As *Temporalität*,
temporality is considered in its function of the condition of the
possibility of the understanding of being (ibid.). Being, in effect, is
intelligible only insofar as it is articulated in reference to time. For
since temporality is the condition of the possibility of Dasein and
since being is articulated in Dasein's own stances, the articulation
of being is done in temporal terms.

In what sense are we to understand the claim that being is articulated in terms of *Temporalität?* Let us focus, with Heidegger, upon
the being of *equipment*. To be a piece of equipment is to belong to
an equipmental totality (thus the hammer, the nails, the bench, etc.,

belong to the workshop of the shoemaker) and thus to stand in a number of functional relations. Hence, when a piece of equipment is understood by us, it is grasped in all the wealth of its functions and functional ties with other items of equipmental totality. Of such "letting function, as *understanding of functionality*" (*BPP* 293), Heidegger will say that it "has a temporal constitution" (ibid.). The point is familiar from and consistent with *Being and Time*. The being of equipment implies that equipment's belonging to the everyday world of practical concerns. Now there is a world for Dasein only insofar as all of the items Dasein encounters are arranged within a temporal framework established by the horizonal schemata (*BPP* 302). This is why Dasein's understanding of the being of equipment occurs within a temporal horizon. All of this is a repetition of the doctrine from *Being and Time*.

But there is also a new point to be considered. To the extent to which human temporality is taken as already determined by its horizonal schemata, it is Temporality (*Temporalität*): "The temporality which is thus primarily carried away to the horizonal schemata of temporality as conditions of the possibility of the understanding of being, constitutes the content of the general concept of Temporality; *Temporality is temporality with regard to the unity of the horizonal schemata belonging to it*" (*BPP* 307). In still another passage Heidegger goes even so far as to *identify* Temporality with the horizonal schema of temporality: he speaks, quite unambiguously, of "the horizonal schema of temporality, Temporality" (*BPP* 312). But then we confront at once the following difficulty. If—as was clearly the case in *Being and Time* and as it continues to be the case in *Basic Problems of Phenomenology*—the horizonal schemata (*Temporalität*) are the interpretations of temporal (*zeitlich*) ecstases onto the *world,* and if the world as a whole collapses in anxiety, then *Temporalität* must lose its significance for the anxious Dasein. There is nothing to suggest that this is *not,* in the end, Heidegger's position. But neither are we told in clear terms that this is his position. Even his insistence that *Temporalität* is derived from *Zeitlichkeit* as from its source or basis[5] is still too vague, for we are not told that the (anxious) grasp of the original temporality as *Zeitlichkeit* undercuts our participation in the (already schematized onto the world) temporality as *Temporalität*. What we can say is that any suggestion to the contrary would be squarely incompatible with the main body of Heidegger's analytic of Dasein. In effect—and to repeat our main point—if anxiety undercuts Dasein's insertion into the world, and if *Temporalität* is bound up with the world, then an anxious Dasein, in discovering the insignificance of the world, must also discover the insignificance of *Temporalität;* and, what is even more important, Dasein must rise to this discovery through the very same stance through which it is brought face-to-face with the finitude of its own *Zeitlichkeit.*

I will conclude by responding to the question I have been asking all along. In my judgment Heidegger does have a powerful and convincing account of the finitude of human time. But he is then unable to reconstruct the connection between time's finitude—the finitude that stems and can only stem from man's sense of inescapable exposure to the violence of death—and the ordinary, commonsensical understanding of time shared by men as they search for a measure of security in life.

In the last sections of his opus magnum Heidegger takes up the task of examining Hegel's views on time and spirit. The task is imposed by the subject matter itself. As Heidegger concedes (*BT* 457), the Hegelian spirit (*Geist*) is inherently temporal. But is *Geist's* temporality the same as the temporality of Dasein? Heidegger thinks not. As he sees it (*BT* 480), Hegel was still imprisoned within the traditional, "ordinary" notion of time. If, then, *Geist* is temporal, and if the time at issue—the only time Heidegger thinks Hegel was familiar with—is time as ordinarily understood, then the temporality of the Hegelian spirit cannot in any way depart from the ordinary model of time.

In the second volume of Hegel's *Encyclopaedia of the Philosophical Sciences* Heidegger finds abundant evidence in support of his interpretation. In the *Encyclopaedia,* time and space are dealt with in the section on Mechanics—a fact significant in itself—and they are conceptualized with the aid of the category of Quantity. Hegel's full justification of this approach is spelled out in the *Science of Logic* (*SL* 187–199), but the outlines of the entire theory can be found as far back as the writings of the Jena period.

Since time and space have the conceptual structure of quantity, both of them exhibit the two moments of that category: continuity and discreteness. However, the way in which continuity and discreteness are related to each other in space differs significantly from their relationship in time. Already in his Jena system Hegel pointed out the difference: "Space is the immediately existing quantity, the concept in itself or as immediate, or in the element of indifference and externality of its moments. [To say that] the difference has abandoned space means: it has ceased to be this indifference, it is for itself in all its restlessness, it is not paralyzed any more . . . This pure quantity as the pure difference existing for itself is . . . time."[6] Now when Hegel says that space is quantity in the form of immediacy and externality he is advancing a claim that will underlie his later criticisms of Kant's Second Antinomy. Quantity, Hegel will argue at length in the *Science of Logic,* must be conceived in such a way that continuity and discreteness are not set apart as mutually incompatible. Kant's antinomy arises only because we start out by implicitly defining each moment of quantity as exclusive of its opposite. The antinomical results are then a foregone conclusion. Now space—or, to be more precise, space when thought of in separation from time—is the privileged illustration of such antinomical conception of quantity. Space, for Hegel, is an indeterminate medium of externally related parts. This is why in space continuity and discreteness cannot be reconciled. "Space is within itself the contradiction of indifferent asunderness and differenceless continuity" (*Enc.* II, par. 260). The unity of these two moments can be recovered only if space is thought of in its connection with time. For time represents a more adequate relationship of continuity and discreteness. And this advantage of time—an advantage space inherits by being bound up with time—is due to time's formal structure as the *negation of a negation.*

The negation—of space, in this case—is the *point.*[7] Since space is an indeterminate manifold, and since determinateness belongs to being and thought alike, space demands of itself some minimum of determinateness. Thus the first and poorest determination of space is the point. A point is, on the one hand, determinate, for it sets itself apart from all of space; but a point's determinateness is, on the other hand, of a most abstract kind, since it is as yet not enriched by a wealth of relations and connections with other parts of space. Such relations and connections emerge only through time. Time as the negation of the negation determines the point as both distinct from and continuous with other points. For, first, as quantity in the state of indifference and externality, space has no fixed *order*. The ordering of parts of space (and thus also the ordering of points, since points, even though posited as negations of space, are still set *in* it[8]) is the work of time.[9] Hence, it is only due to space's bond with time that a point comes to occupy a distinct place in an ordered sequence of points. Let us consider two points *A* and *B*. To say that *A* is prior to *B* means that *A* comes earlier than *B* in the temporal emergence of a line being drawn between *A* and *B*. Second, a point becomes continuous with other points only when connected with them through the temporal process of constructing a determinate line or figure. Only thus can a point be established as "belonging together" with other points in the unity of a spatial whole. Now since space must reach the stage of concrete determinateness--both in order and in continuity—and since such a determinateness of space emerges from temporal processes, time is the *truth* of space (*Enc.* II, par. 257, Zusatz). The separation of space from time must be rejected as a product of a one-sided and incomplete conception to the extent to which space *fulfills* itself in time. Conversely, too, time cannot be separated from space. For time's basic elements—the Nows—are fleeting and vanishing; they may be retained *subjectively* in a recollection, but their *objective* existence must be fixed in space. It is thus incorrect to talk—as Kant still did, at least in the *Transcendental Aesthetic*—of time and of space as of two different forms of intuition; rather, space and time must be seen as moments of one and the same whole of space-time (ibid) in which "the spatial aspect presents itself as the form of indifferent juxtaposition and quiescent subsistence; the temporal aspect, on the other hand presents itself as the form of unrest, of the immanently negative, of successiveness, of arising and vanishing" (*Enc.* III, par. 448, Zusatz).

No extended commentary is needed to justify Heidegger's claim that time as Hegel describes it in the *Encyclopaedia* is indeed—in Heidegger's terminology—time as "ordinarily" understood. In effect, Hegel's analyses bring out what constitutes, for Heidegger, the most abstract and poorest form of the ordinary conception of time: time as a homogeneous sequence of Nows. To be sure, in Hegel this sequence is not conceptualized with the aid of the abstract categories of *Verstand,* unable to think the unity of continuity and discreteness. Still, from the Heideggerian point of view, Hegel's main contribution boils down to a mere improvement upon the ordinary conception of time as a series of Nows.

The formal definition of time given by Hegel in the Encyclopaedia—time "is Becoming (*Werden*) directly intuited" (*Enc.* II, par. 258)—gives Heidegger an additional opening for pushing his main criticism. If time is *intuited* Becoming, then time turns out to be made up of a collection of present-at-hand items (the Nows). But then, as Heidegger points out (*BT* 483), the future and the past are conceived as being only the "now that is not yet" and the "now that is no longer." The "now" is thus "monstrously privileged" (ibid.), and this, for Heidegger, is the most striking feature of the ordinary conception of time (in sharp contrast with the temporality of Dasein, defined by the priority of the future).

However, the next item in Heidegger's case against Hegel is much harder to accept. According to Heidegger, the life of the Hegelian *Geist* is indeed temporal, but the time in which *Geist* unfolds itself does not differ significantly from time as ordinarily understood. In effect—this is the main support Heidegger marshals in favor of the present stage of his criticism of Hegel—spirit can deploy itself in time only because spirit too is the *negation of a negation,* that is, only because the formal structure of spirit is identical with the structure of time as *ordinarily* understood (*BT* 485).

The proposition that spirit is the negation of a negation is, of course, one of the basic tenets of Hegel's philosophy. Spirit is the negation of a negation to the extent that the life of spirit means the abolition of externally related elements and their sublation into an organized whole. For example, an individual self negates the separateness of its own representations and desires and raises them to the level of a holistic unity of spiritual experience. This is what the activity and the development of spirit are all about. Hence the formal principle of spirit is indeed the same as the formal principle of time; Hegel reminds us of this in the very same section of the *Encyclopaedia* in which he develops the main body of his doctrine of time: "Time is the same principle as the $I = I$ of pure self-consciousness" (*Enc.* II, par. 258, Remark). But while Hegel *does* say that the principle of the I is the same as the principle of time, he also says—in the same sentence—that time is "this principle, or the simple Notion still in its *uttermost externality and abstraction* [my italics], as intuited mere *Becoming*" (ibid.). It seems, then, that the negation of a negation as embodied in the life of spirit may yet turn out to be radically different from the negation of a negation represented by time—or at least by the sort of time Hegel was dealing with in the *Encyclopaedia's* section on Mechanics. But this possibility would entail consequences incompatible with the main thrust of Heidegger's criticism of Hegel. Heidegger writes: "Because the restlessness with which *spirit* develops in bringing itself to its concept is the *negation of a negation,* it accords with spirit, as it actualizes itself, to fall 'into *time*' as the immediate *negation of a negation*" (*BT* 485). But in this crucial passage Heidegger seems to be begging the question. For even though spirit and time are both negations of a negation, only time is the immediate form of such a negation of a negation: in contrast, the *immediate* form of the negation of a negation does not characterize the life of *spirit.* Of course, the unfolding of spirit must still take place in time (*PhM* 800). But it then follows that the time of spiritual life will have to be completely different from the sort of time we have become familiar with from Hegel's analyses in the section on Mechanics. Is it possible to find in Hegel such a different conception of time?

The affirmative answer to this question is at the foundation of Kojève's entire interpretation of Hegel. Moreover, as Kojève readily acknowledges (*ILH* 367), a good deal of his argument is based on a well-known article by Koyré,[10] in which Koyré credits Hegel with the discovery—in the Jena writings of 1802—of human temporality deployed, as in Heidegger, through man's projection toward the future. Heidegger, Koyré writes in still another article,[11] didn't seem to be aware of his kinship with Hegel. His criticisms of Hegel, therefore, inevitably miss the mark: they are valid with respect to the notion of time worked out in the Hegelian *Mechanics,* but they do not apply to Hegel's conception of the temporality of spirit—the temporality of acts through which spirit posits its determinate forms and shapes only to transcend them again through its own striving. When Hegel is concerned with the temporality of spirit he clearly shifts away from the (ordinary) time of the "correlata"[12] of spiritual acts and he attempts to describe "the autoconstitution of time,"[13] or, more precisely, "the constitution or autoconstitution of the concept of time."[14] Koyré's terminology here is Husserlian, and purposely so, since the implicit comparison with Husserl's *Vorlesungen zur Phänomenologie des inneren Zeitbewusstseins* is meant to emphasize Hegel's concern with the temporality of *consciousness*. And *this* form of time, as Hegel himself was fully aware, cannot be grasped with the aid of the category of quantity,[15] which supplies the conceptual framework for the analyses of time carried out in the second volume of the *Encyclopaedia*.

Hegel, Koyré thinks,[16] was led onto the discovery of the temporality of consciousness through his interest in the notion of Life. Hegel defines the human self as *conscious life,* as ''genus for itself'' (*PhM* 224). Now life for Hegel—his position has not changed much from his early writings to the works of his maturity—exhibits the pattern of Infinity. Life is the restlessness of an absolute unity positing itself in differences and then returning from them again to itself. This is not the ''bad'' infinity of abstract thinking—the *schlechte Unendlichkeit*—set apart from all differences, but the infinity of a self-moving totality which expresses itself in all the details of the empirical world. When conceptualized in the Hegelian fashion, the infinity of life exhibits several moments that reemerge—raised to the level of self-consciousness—in a human self.

Our immediate perception of life gives us its first and most abstract moment: individual animals and plants considered in the separateness of their here and now, in their mere ''particularity.'' The moment of particularity is by no means a mere illusion, hiding behind it some differenceless identity of life as a whole. Nevertheless—and this is the second moment of life's infinity—the living particulars assert their separateness only to have it dissolved again in the general substance of life. This is what the very ''process'' (*PhM* 223) of life is all about: an individual organism sustains itself in order to give birth to its offspring and then dies. In this way the ''universality'' of life reasserts its claims against the separateness of individuals. ''Thus both the sides of the entire movement which were before distinguished, viz., the *setting up of individual forms* lying apart and undisturbed in the universal medium of independent existence, and the process of life—collapse into one another'' (*PhM* 223–224). When Hegel talks about life as ''genus'' (ibid.) he refers to the unity of the two moments of life.[17]

Now—and this is Koyré's main point—when life gains its conscious level in a human self (''genus for itself''), the movement of life takes up the form of temporalizing. In effect, what life as such is doing to (merely) living individuals, a human self does to itself. For a human self just *is* a restless activity of first positing itself in determinate forms and then surpassing and changing them through its own efforts. The change is here entirely self-induced and self-generated: a human individual is in a state of perpetual disquietude and striving, and this state is at the source of a constant transformation an individual imposes upon himself.

In order to emerge as capable of such self-transormation, an individual must be able to break his ties with the past. Or, to put it in more technical terms, the causal explanation of human choices and actions must be repudiated in favor of a view attributing to man a freedom from his past. But—and we are coming here to the core of human temporality as Koyré interprets it in his article—in order to be able to free himself from the causal chains binding him to his past, man must live in a present that is *exclusive* of the past; in the present, that is, whose utter simplicity and autonomy[18] allows man to make his choices independently of whatever his past is or might have been.

Still, this utter simplicity of the present is only one aspect of the complex structure of the human present. For in order to negate and to surpass my established condition I must have some sense of where I want to go and what I want to achieve. Were I to be completely locked within the present slice of my mental life I would have no vision of things as they might be—that is, other than what they actually are—and so I wouldn't even entertain the mere idea of changing my condition. Only my glance into some as yet unfulfilled possibilities (into the future) can invite the change; it is thus the future that destabilizes the present. Insofar, then, as the human present is the present of (self-induced) change and modification, it cannot be separated from the future.[19]

Since human temporality is the process of man's self-induced transformation, and since this process takes off with the disclosure of some unfulfilled possibilities posited by the self, the temporality of consciousness, Koyré notes,[20] shows a clear priority of the future. The similarity with the Heideggerian temporality of Dasein is obvious. But we can push this comparison even further than Koyré himself does. The comparison is suggested both by Hegel's overall argument and by his quite specific statements: "this future is not in fact the *future* [my italics], it is rather what sublates the present and . . . it is rather the present which is, in conformity with its essence, the nonbeing of itself, i.e., the future."[21] The future, that is—or at least the sort of future disclosed in *human* temporalizing—is not to be viewed as being "later" than the present. The future is actual and actually given in the present to the extent that the present would not be what it is—a break with the past—without being shaped by a sense of at least some possibilities open to the self.

I have said that the future *destabilizes* the present. But, on the other hand, this very process of the future destabilizing the present and breaking the latter's bonds with the past amounts to the *re-emergence of the past*—albeit in a new and changed function. For the struggle between "the new" and "the old" must come to some (even if only partial and provisional) resolution. And this resolution is the past.[22] Let us explain this paradox. Departing from his present and acting upon his vision of the future, man comes to *achieve* something. From now on, these achievements will always be behind him; while he still will be able to deny their worth or importance, he will not be able to act as if they were not *his* achievements, as if they didn't *define* him. He can still change his way of living. But whatever he aims at accomplishing, he must take into account what he has accomplished so far. The past is thus integrated into the present insofar as man's activity of self-transformation takes place within a set of conditions which are—to a significant degree—the results of his own previous actions. And this actuality of the past is—again—very similar to what we have learned on this subject from Heidegger's phenomenology. For in Hegel, too, the human past cannot be seen as something merely left behind and irrelevant to the present. In both Hegel and Heidegger the past—or at least the *human* past—is very much alive in the present, since it supplies the background of all human creativity.

With the reemergence of the past in the present the unity of all three dimensions of time is recovered—the unity was never really lost, to be more precise, since the independence of the present from the future and from the past was only a (one-sided) aspect of their full relationship—and this is what gives us time as a whole: "the once (*das Ehmals*) itself is not for itself, it is equally the present moment which transforms itself into its opposite through the future and which is not separated from those two; in itself, it is only the entire circuit, the real (*reale*) time which through the present moment and the future becomes the once."[23]

But this reemergence of the past in the (future-oriented) present is implied not only by the overall structure of time. It is also—and above anything else—required as the most fundamental condition of the possibility of the life of spirit. For spirit can grow and develop only by internalizing its past experiences, by making them part and parcel of its living present. And this phenomenon represents perhaps the most profound difference between *human* temporality, and time as we find it *outside* of the area of human experiences. When the integrated totality of temporal dimensions is posited as existing outside and independently of human experiences, it loses at once its entire wholeness and unity. The dimensions of time become then external and indifferent to each other; the past cannot be preserved in and enriching the present since—given the absence of a human self's recollections—there is nothing that retains and keeps the past alive. In this way time falls into indifference and externality of space.[24] When thus *spatialized,* the past is embodied only in physical marks or traces—an old building, a ghost-town, etc.—which cannot even be understood *as past* without a reference to human records and recollections. Once again, Hegel's position turns out to be remarkably close to Heidegger's, since for Heidegger, too, space is accessible to human experiences only on the grounds of time.[25]

But do all these similarities between Hegel and Heidegger add up to the conclusion both Koyré and Kojève subscribe to? Was it really Hegel—and not Heidegger—who first went beyond the ordinary conception of time and grounded it in the finite temporality of man?

Let us note immediately that the Hegelian description of the time of consciousness as we have just tried to summarize it does not, in any case, take us further than what Heidegger calls the *in*authentic temporality. The restlessness and the relentlessness of spirit's self-overcoming are, in fact, the very same qualities that we found in the inauthentic Dasein's feverish pursuit of its transient goals. But a conception of the *in*authentic temporality is not sufficient to discover and to overcome the limitations of the ordinary model of time. On the contrary, as we remember from our earlier discussion of Heidegger, the inauthentic temporality—the temporality of a Dasein bent on making the world a safe place to live—defines itself by the absorption in the world and, therefore, by the adoption of some form of the ordinary model of time.

Are we justified, though, in claiming that Hegel was familiar—at the very best—only with the inauthentic form of human temporality? Kojève's entire interpretation can be seen as sustained by an effort to reply negatively to this question. For, Kojéve thinks, in Hegel the striving of the human self springs from its responses—in *Desire,* in *Labor* and in attitudes taken toward *Death*—to the inescapable finitude of the human condition. And this claim—if correct—links up Hegel with Heidegger in a way that makes the two philosophers' positions on time essentially identical.

However, in what follows I shall be arguing that neither Desire, nor Labor, nor Death, as conceptualized by Hegel, can bring us close to the notion of finite temporality in the Heideggerian sense of that term.

Desire

Desire is temporal, for it is a striving, and a striving not to be confused with a specific and determinate need. But neither is desire to be conceived as a vague longing of the soul—the *Sehnsucht* of the Romantics. For desire expresses itself in *action.* And when action emerges as the vehicle of desire, it organizes itself in the form of temporality. Now if action is "born of desire" (*ILH* 11), and if desire imposes upon action the form of temporality, then the Heideggerian *dictum* that temporality is "the meaning of Dasein's being as care" may apply equally well to the Hegelian *Geist.*

But what is desire? How does it differ from specific needs and appetites? On what grounds do we want to claim that human actions are sustained—in one way or another—by the striving of desire? And, above all, if desire is temporal, what kind of temporality is it?

To begin with, then, there can be no doubt that desire, its special status notwithstanding, must have a foundation in our biological needs and appetites. As a desiring self, man is first of all a *living* self. Hegel talks about it a great deal in the *Encyclopaedia (Enc.* III, par. 426, Zusatz), but in the *Phenomenology of Mind*—the work around which Kojève builds the bulk of his interpretation—his position is equally clear. Since the subject of desire is always a living self (albeit not fully self-conscious yet but only in the process of gaining self-consciousness), desire cannot be separated from a background of man's natural appetites, drives, and needs. Furthermore, the relation between those appetites, needs, etc., on the one hand, and desire, on the other hand, is not a relation of mere externality. For desire is, first and foremost, a felt *lack (Enc.* III, par.

427, Zusatz); now, if the self were not *defined* by its needs and appetites, it would represent a self-sufficient and self-enclosed realm, and then nothing would be able to move the self to desire this or that. However, if the emergence of desire is inconceivable except in the context of biological needs and appetites, the latter are by no means *sufficient* to account for the emergence of desire and for its main features. For desire erupts when mere need and appetition are subsumed under conceptions and meanings of spirit. Hegel sometimes vacillates on this issue,[26] but Kojève—with a greater consistency than Hegel himself, it seems to me—goes to great pains to emphasize that the specifically *human* desire is always shot through with a conception and a purpose that cannot possibly be accounted for in merely biological terms (*ILH* 11–12).

Of this conception and of this purpose always present in human desire Hegel himself offers a detailed description in the *Phenomenology of Mind* (*PhM* 225–226). Desire is at first—in its form of a mere *Begierde*—an immediate, unthinking drive of self-consciousness to confirm its "infinity." Self-consciousness, let us recall, emerges in the *Phenomenology* at the end of the section on Understanding (*Verstand*). In the final stages of that section the self comes to realize that reality is not to be viewed as made up of some independent entities or laws set over against the self's experiences. The self recognizes reality as its own reflection, an extension of itself, as it were. And this recognition—a watershed in the development of consciousness' self-interpretation—supplies the ground for the self's immediate faith ("certainty") in being the center of the whole of reality. The dawn of desire is thus the eruption of a self's narcissism, of its unshakable faith in its right and its ability to enclose all of reality within its own boundaries.

The self, however, cannot remain in such a blissful *state* of self-contentment. It must set out to *confirm* its narcissism, and this the self does by letting loose against reality all of its needs and appetites. Since reality is interpreted as being merely the extension of the self, the self treats its entire environment as a field of private satisfactions. Everywhere the self must leave its own stamp by bringing reality under the sway of its unrestrained appetites and needs.

A contradiction can be seen to emerge at once. The self's claim is infinite and universal (to be the center of the *whole* of reality), but its appetitive satisfactions are merely finite and particular (the

self assimilates either this or that, *or*—if it spreads itself still further—this *and* that, but then *not* something still other and still out-
standing, etc.). The self aims at permanence (of its victory over
reality's resistance), but it achieves only instantaneity (of a momentary satisfaction of appetite). The purpose of the self was to
raise itself (to the mastery of nature), but it sees itself debased (to
the level of a merely natural self, preoccupied by its crude needs
and appetites). If we sum up these failures of *Begierde,* we can say
that the self was aiming at the life of self-sufficiency and finality;
yet it has achieved only the dependency and the transitoriness of a
merely appetitive life. And this contradiction between the goal and
the result mobilizes the self to an additional—and equally spurious—burst of activity. The activity the self will now display—in
trying to extend its appetites over more and more items—is bound
to be a spurious one, since the goal pursued by the self can in no
way be realized through the satisfaction of natural needs and
appetites.

The contradiction Hegel discovers in *Begierde* is the point of
departure of Kojève's entire interpretation of the Hegelian theory of
desire—and indeed of Hegel's *Phenomenology* as a whole. Hegel
himself points the way. The *truth* of desire is a "reduplication of
self-consciousness" (*PhM* 226) since, as Kojève expounds on
Hegel's thought, "in truth" (i.e., in point of fact, implicitly) a
self's desire is the desire of another self (*ILH* 13). This explains
both why desire in its first and immediate form of a mere *Begierde*
is torn by a contradiction *and* why the fulfillment of desire can only
be achieved in satisfying man's desire of (and for) another human
self. When taken jointly, these two claims will supply the premises
of Kojève's account of human temporality in terms of desire.

The underlying cause of the contradictory outcome of *Begierde*—and the first sense in which the desire for another self is
the "truth" of any human desire—is the fact that the desire of and
for another self is the very *condition of the possibility* of human
desire as such. Desire, in effect, is always intentional; it is always
desire *of* or *for* something; desire is thus determined by what and
how it desires. Now if desire is determined by the object it aims
at—or to be more precise, by that object as it is represented through
a certain conception the desiring self has of it—and if, as we recall,
the object of desire is pursued by man to give him a sense of independence and autonomy, then it follows, Kojève concludes (*ILH*

12, 168), that the implicit target of desire cannot be a merely *natural* object but only another human self with all of its (specifically human) qualities of spirituality and freedom. For only as a self desiring (be it implicitly and unconsciously) another self can I rise to the level of desire—of a fully *human* desire—in which I do not succumb to the dependency and heteronomy of merely natural appetites and needs.

Furthermore, if desire is implicitly the desire of another self, then it is a longing and a striving which goes beyond what is merely *given*. For that other self—the self desired and searched for—is not *itself* something merely given. The self is defined by the power—the self's negativity, its freedom—of asserting itself against all of its concrete determinations. This is why such a free self has the ever-present capacity of refusing to succumb to any pressures and obligations imposed upon it by another self. Hence to desire a human self is to go after something that is in principle elusive and forever beyond one's control. This is what imparts to desire its quality of infinite striving. And this striving is the temporality of desire (*ILH* 12, 367).

Now if desire is in fact or implicitly the desire of another self (the first sense in which desire of another self is the "truth" of every specifically human desire), then the only path along which desire can reach its goal is the path leading to one's fulfillment through relations with another self (the second sense in which desire of another self is the "truth" of all human desires). A desiring self reaches its adequate satisfaction by finding acceptance in another self. Hegel's term for this acceptance is "acknowledgment" or "recognition" (*Anerkennung*). The final goal of human desire is thus, Kojève concludes (*ILH* 14, 368), the achievement of recognition.

In the striving of desire, Kojève discovers the structure typical of human temporality. Like the temporality of Dasein, the temporality of the desiring self exhibits a clear priority of the future (*ILH* 367). The future, in effect, is above all else something as yet unfulfilled, something delineated only in the imagination and the anticipation of the agent. But such is precisely the initial status of the desired state of recognition—of the acknowledgment of a self by other selves. For this acknowledgment, too, is not something given but something to be first created and won over. Hence—if we are prepared to agree with Kojève that desire of recognition is at the root of all human hopes and aspirations—it is the search for

recognition that first gives the self the creative, future-oriented impulse. But, at the same time, this orientation toward the future
springs from the soil of the past. In order to effectively realize new
possibilities I must, of course, change the conditions prevailing at
the time of my action, but I must *also* rely upon those conditions
(upon the materials available, the technology, the inherited practices, etc.) in all of my creative efforts. And so I come *at* the future
from the springboard of the past; I must both know and utilize the
past in order to bring about a new future (*ILH* 369). Finally—and
this, too, is strictly parallel to the Heideggerian temporality of Dasein—the present (the *human* present) is opened up as the last stage
of the circuit future → past → present: "It is the way in which the
Past has been (negatively) formed in terms of the Future that determines the quality of the Present. And it is only the Present thus
determined by the Future and the Past which is a human or historical Present" (*ILH* 368).

　　The analogy with Heidegger, however, breaks down as soon as
we take a closer look at the sort of future desire aims at. For if in the
temporality of desire the future enjoys a clear priority over the past
and the present, and if the meaning of the future envisioned by the
desiring self is the state of recognition and acceptance by other
selves, then the temporality of desire must be considered—from
the Heideggerian point of view—as being inauthentic through and
through. When everything is said and done, the temporality of desire is only the temporality of a self aspiring to achieve *social acceptance*. Such temporality is the exact opposite of a form of
temporalizing through which Dasein is torn away from the public
world and brought face-to-face with its exposure to the violence of
death.

　　It can be pointed out to us immediately that the Hegelian self's
desire of social acceptance ought not to be interpreted as an attempt, by the self, simply to *suppress* its own particularity by subsuming it under some common and abstract quality (of "citizen" or
of "free self-consciousness," etc.). On the contrary—and as
Hegel amply demonstrated in his famous analysis of *Evil and For-
giveness*—an individual wants to be accepted in all the wealth of
his personal passions, desires, preferences, and so on. Far from
being tantamount to the suppression of the self's particularity, the
recognition, when fully unfolded, will in fact allow a human indi-

vidual to acknowledge and to take up the entire content of his personality.

But this suggestion, although perfectly sound, will only contribute to the strengthening of our main point. Let us only take a closer look at the meaning of the full acceptance of the self's particular content. An individual who refuses to grant such an acceptance to others adopts the attitude of a "beautiful soul" (*schöne Seele*)—he withdraws from the world of action and persists in an outright condemnation of that world as a place ruled by merely private passions and desires of active individuals. The target of the beautiful soul's condemnations is the man of action. The latter is constantly *judged* by the former, and the judgments issued by the beautiful soul focus only upon the particular aspects of human actions. Thus (*PhM* 672), if some deeds bring glory to the agent, the judge—the beautiful soul—*explains* the agent's dedication by his vanity; if, again, the man of action rises through his accomplishments above his original station in life, the unyielding judge condemns him as being moved by mere ambition, and so on. Any claim of the man of action to have acted—as he thinks he did—in accordance with his sense of duty is viewed by the beautiful soul as a perfidious exercise in hypocrisy.

Hegel first points out that the judge's attitude leads to a contradiction both in his state of mind and in his behavior. In effect, when condemning the man of action, the beautiful soul has no *public* standards to which it can appeal. However this may displease the beautiful soul, the world persists in bestowing praise upon men of action and achievement; hence, the beautiful soul can judge such men only by "its *own* law" (*PhM* 670). But this is incompatible with the beautiful soul's own better knowledge that moral judgments must be passed and tested in conformity with public standards. Thus, the mental attitude of the beautiful soul is torn apart by two conflicting commitments: on the one hand, the commitment to the inevitably public status of moral judgments and evaluations and, on the other hand, a stubborn attachment to one's own way of evaluating people and their actions (ibid.). The conduct of the beautiful soul is equally contradictory. For the judge realizes that a true dedication to duty must be expressed in action; yet he shuns the world of action and drifts away into passive contemplation. If, then, the man of action is to be viewed as hypocritical—on the grounds that he claims to act out of his sense of duty while in fact he is bent on gratifying his passions—so too is the judge (*PhM* 671).

In point of fact, however, the situation of the beautiful soul is much less fruitful than that of the active individual in at least two closely related respects. First, the man of action has at least some *impact* upon the world, while the beautiful soul drifts into irrelevance and, conscious of the contradiction of its commitments, "runs to madness, wastes itself in yearning, and pines away in consumption" (*PhM* 676). More important, it is precisely the implacable judge who proves to be truly *base* in his attitude. For his is the attitude of a valet toward the hero whom he serves: the valet sees the hero in his mundane, daily preoccupations and idiosyncrasies, and he has no eyes for the hero's greatness. Not because, Hegel insists (*PhM* 673), the hero is not a hero but because the valet is a valet.

Seeing through the hypocrisies of the judge, the man of action *confesses* to his ambition and his search for glory and expects a corresponding confession from the beautiful soul. On this basis, the man of action hopes, "the state of mutual recognition will be brought about" (*PhM* 674). The first impulse of the judge, hardened in his self-righteousness, will be to refuse to acknowledge his similarity with the man of action and to dismiss the latter's confession as one more exercise in insincerity. If and when the judge acknowledges the commonality of predicament binding him with the man of action, the Hegelian recognition will have unfolded its full potential: the two individuals will come to accept each other as *concretely universal,* that is, as universal in all the particularities of their passions, needs, and desires. When those passions, needs, and desires are put in service of ethical purposes, there is no contradiction between an individual's pursuit of his own gratification and his dedication to duty. For this reason, "the word of reconciliation is the *objectively existent spirit,* which immediately apprehends the pure knowledge of itself *qua* universal essence in its opposite . . . a reciprocal recognition which is Absolute Spirit" (*PhM* 677; my italics).

This quotation allows us to measure the distance separating, at this point, Hegel and Heidegger. While the Hegelian recognition does indeed embrace the particularity of the self, it also brings that particularity within the public world. But, as we saw so many times, the Heideggerian *Angst* opens up an unbridgeable gap between an individual and his public world. And, for this reason, the temporality of a self striving to achieve the Hegelian recognition will be radically different from the temporality of anxiety as we encountered it earlier in this chapter when analyzing the positions of Heidegger.

The everyday Dasein lives in a *public* time (*BT* 469; *BPP* 264). This means, to begin with, that every "now" of the ordinary chronology is immediately understood by all members of the public realm. While, says Heidegger (*BPP* 264), different persons may date the same now by reference to a different event—to some of them a given now may mean "now, that it is time to go to work," to others (working a night shift) the same now may signify the end of the working time—all persons involved have in view one and the same moment of the temporal chronology. This publicness of time is secured by the common rhythm of life underlying the endeavors of all members of the community. It is not the case that each individual first lives in his own stream of temporal experiences and then descends to the level of public time: "the publicness of time is . . . rooted in the ecstatic-horizonal character of temporality" (*BPP* 270). Since, as we remember from our earlier analyses, temporality is schematized onto the world and since the world is public, the everyday time is shared by all of us. But, for the same reason, the publicness of time is suspended by anxiety. For anxiety sets an individual apart from his public world and hence also apart from the shared framework of world-time. In contrast, the temporal striving of the Hegelian self is the very process through which this self unfolds its potential as the vehicle of the universal *Geist:* "Time . . . appears as the spirit's destiny and necessity, where spirit is not yet complete within itself; it is the necessity compelling spirit to enrich the share self-consciousness has in consciousness" (*PhM* 800).

But, one could object, isn't it the case that for Hegel the recognition cannot be earned by a cowardly and fearful self unable to risk biological survival in a life-and-death struggle for prestige, honor, or dignity? And if the man searching for recognition must thus be able to endure the experience of the "nothingness of death"[27]—of *his own* death—then how does he differ, at least in this respect, from a Dasein coming to terms with its own finitude? And how can we then claim that in Hegel the temporality of desire—the tem-

porality of a self willing and capable to endure the thought of its
own finitude—ought to be lumped together with the "inauthentic"
temporality of a Dasein bent on concealing and covering up its
finitude?

These important questions shift the focus of our discussion.
They won't be answered until we have become clear about the
meaning and the status of death in the experiences of a Hegelian
self. *Does* the sense of death, in Hegel, amount to the disclosure of
a self's finitude? We shall take this question up in a later section of
the present chapter.

Labor

On Kojève's reading of Hegel (*ILH* 167, 371), labor represents
one of the two main paths (the struggle being the other one) along
which desire moves toward its ultimate goal of recognition. The
path of labor is not taken *voluntarily*. In contrast with the struggle—in which an individual makes a free decision to risk his life
for the sake of prestige, honor, and dignity—the activity of labor is
a *forced* activity. To be sure, the status of a forced laborer (the
slave) is imposed upon the individual as a result of a *prior* free
decision of his own: the decision to abandon the fight for honor and
dignity and to opt for mere survival instead. When once made,
however, the decision to quit the struggle amounts to the subjection
of the one who made it to the power of natural causation in general.
His attachment to survival will allow his victorious adversary to
gain mastery and control over him.

The purpose of self-consciousness as such is to establish the
self's dominion over the world. This purpose the victorious self
(the master) now pursues by forcing labor upon the self vanquished
in the struggle. Due to the labor of slaves, the long process toward
human dominion over nature takes off—in the short run, to the
benefit of slave owners, in the long run, though, to the benefit of
man as a species.

Considered as the activity of the laboring self, labor is desire
repressed and postponed. First, in the simple and obvious sense that
the strenuous effort of the laboring self is expended on supplying
enjoyments to *another self;* the agent of labor is thus separated from
the fruits of his own activity. Second, and more important, labor is
desire postponed in the sense that the ultimate goal of desire—

recognition—is now established as the final station of a long and painful journey through which the laboring part of humanity slowly creates the conditions (both social and natural) for extracting recognition from the masters.

As desire repressed and postponed, labor is considered only in its *negative* function. Labor's *positive* function—its function of being the self-formative activity of man—allows us to discover the *temporality* of labor in all its originality and distinctness from other forms of human temporalizing. First, it must be noted in this connection, that in its positive function of transforming man and man's immediate natural environment, labor is the only activity capable of bringing about *real* changes in the very materiality of the world. Hegel was elaborating on this theme from the Jena system[28] to the writing of his mature period (*SL* 746): in labor, a human agent does violence to nature by unleashing against it the very natural forces which are arrayed against him. By this "ruse of reason" (*List der Vernunft*)—by cleverly using wind and water and fire to implement his own purposes—man changes beyond recognition the face of the earth. And these man-induced changes are the precipitates of the temporality of labor: "It is the human labor that *temporalizes* the natural, spatial World" (*ILH* 377). Hence the temporality of labor—and it alone—offers man a chance to objectify and objectively realize his own impulse of creating a *new* (i.e., specifically human) future. As we saw earlier, the *human* future is not something fixed in the order of things; it first emerges in the creative imagination and conception of human agents; it is, to begin with, something not yet given, something radically new with respect to the way things are and have been until now. And this future in the strong and genuine sense of the term—the only *consistently* used sense of the term, since the future resembling the past would not take us beyond the ontology of the eternal return of the same—can be more than a subjective fancy, more than a dream, only because man realizes it through his labor. "It is Labor and Labor only which transforms the World in an *essential* manner, by creating truly new realities" (*ILH* 376).

By transforming the world in conformity with human ideas and conceptions labor achieves in practice what the traditional epistemology was not able to achieve in theory. Through labor, being and thought are brought together. "[T]he phase of inherent existence (*Ansichsein*) or thinghood, which received its form and shape through labor, is no other substance than consciousness" (*PhM* 242). Thus our conceptions "correspond"—if that is still the word—to external reality, because the latter is not to be construed as a collection of independent entities but as a man-made environment shaped in conformity with the very same conceptions and ideas that make up the inventory of our conceptual scheme. Even Kant, Kojève argues,[29] was still unable to give an account of that unity of conception and reality, since for Kant Intuition—both in its form and in its content—is merely *given* to Understanding (hence all the dualisms that Kant was, in the end, unable to resolve). The resolution ought not to be searched for in some hypothetically posited mechanisms of "transcendental imagination." The resolution is supplied by the world-making powers of human labor. In labor, the gulf between thought and being disappears: both of them are aspects of one and the same process through which man makes and remakes himself and his environment.

If the temporality of labor is human creativity objectifying itself and achieving permanence—in the man-made world of human institutions and of "humanized" nature—and if man's creative impulse is, as we noted earlier, fueled by desire's goal of achieving recognition and acceptance by other selves, then this ultimate purpose of desire is brought closer and objectively secured with the growth of the labor-created world. Labor creates the soil in which the ideals pursued by desire can flourish and endure. This, for Kojève,[30] is the greatest originality and the greatest advantage of labor over that other path toward recognition: the struggle for prestige. In effect, even a victorious struggle for prestige does not embody itself in a permanent setting: the victor has his "moment of triumph," but it is a brief moment indeed, and an unproductive one at that. Hence the lot of the Hegelian master is to exhaust himself in the life of decadence and of merely private enjoyment (*PhM* 236). In contrast, the laborer gives to his slowly emerging worth an objective and permanent form: in the skills and the education that he has acquired, in the changes he has imposed upon nature, in the evolving social institutions and so on. The pride that the laborer can take in himself—and the recognition that he will soon extract from the master—are enshrined in the enduring edifice of the public world.

On account of labor's *forced* character—the slave is compelled to work by the ever-present threat of his master's sword—this self-formative activity of man emerges as an external necessity in which he does not recognize himself. And this has important consequences for man's interpretation of the temporality of labor.

Let us first point out the obvious: labor "takes time"; the transformation of both the external environment and of the laborer himself is a long and painful process. The resistance and the inertia of crude nature—both outside and inside man—do not give way instantenously and all at once. "Labor *is* Time and this is why it is necessarily *in* time: it demands time" (*ILH* 180). Labor-Time is "in" time in the sense in which the Heideggerian temporality of Dasein's activity "expresses" itself in the (chronologically determined) time of the work world. Now, as long as man (man as Kojève finds him described in Hegel's phenomenology under the name of "spirit") does not recognize his own creativity in the process of labor, the time that labor "takes"—the time of changes brought about, one after another, in the human world—will appear to man under the form of an independent and objective chronology (*ILH* 383–384). This illusion of an independent, ready-made time will persist until the Hegelian spirit (i.e., man) reappropriates its own spontaneity (*PhM* 800). The similarities with Heidegger's doctrine of the world-time's unfounded claims to independence are clear.

An objection can immediately be raised against what we just said. For isn't it the case that in Heidegger the falling of Dasein into the public world and its allegedly "objective" time is in fact an *escape* from Dasein's own mortal self? And isn't Hegel's position on the issue the exact opposite of the Heideggerian view to the extent to which the Hegelian self, far from escaping from itself into the public world, fully *realizes* itself in it?

Put in this way, however, the objection is too easy, and it can be refuted easily. For in Hegel, too, the rechanneling of human energies into labor must be seen as a result of some individuals' (the future slaves') inability to overcome the fear of death. Like the inauthentic Dasein, the Hegelian slave chooses the security and the objectivity of the work-world over the danger of a lonely encounter with his own death during the struggle. The temporality of labor is the Hegelian counterpart of the inauthentic temporality of Dasein.

A more difficult question can now be raised. If the self's fearful refusal to come to terms with its own mortality is at the root of the ("inauthentic") temporality of labor, does it follow that the *accep-

tance of one's mortality is tantamount, in Hegel, to the discovery of finite temporality in the Heideggerian sense of that term? This is indeed Kojève's central claim. Can it be substantiated?

Death

The connection of temporality with the self's finitude is by no means something merely superadded to desire and labor. Both desire and labor are future oriented. Now a *human* future can only be disclosed by a *conception* we form of it.[31] Our sense of some as-yet-unfulfilled possibilities can be something real to us and can move us to act only when it is fixed and articulated in a description we give of it to ourselves and to others.[32] However vague and underdetermined that description may be, it can never be lacking altogether if a self—a *human* self—is to have any sense of the future it is aiming at. To the extent, then, that both desire and labor are guided by a vision of a human future, their temporality is already shaped by conception. Now, there is a close link, according to Kojève, between the concept in general and as such (the Hegelian *Begriff*) and human finitude. Or, to put it differently, our ability to ascend to the level of *Begriff* turns out to be linked up with the sense of ourselves as mortal beings. Temporality is thus grounded in human finitude.

Let us explain all this by starting with the simplest cases. *Every* act of subsuming a particular under the corresponding universal concept is—Kojève repeats after Hegel (*ILH* 372)—an act of "murder." To consider this dog as a particular member of the whole class of dogs is to consider him as limited and finite by virtue of his very distinctness from other dogs. But, as Hegel taught us, whatever is limited and finite—whatever is marked off by its determinate boundaries—must go under and pass away. And so my mere grasp of a particular dog as a member of the class of dogs is tantamount to passing a death sentence upon him. The concept endures, but the particular suffers destruction. More than that, the concept subtracts itself from the sway of time (the concept "dog" is passed on from generation to generation), but there *are* concepts only because particulars *do* go under, that is, only because *they* are subject to the sway of time (*ILH* 373).

All of the above must be applied to human selves as well. We couldn't talk about the *concept* of a self unless *particular* selves were finite and mortal. Hegel's argument from Sense-Certainty (*PhM* 154) gives clear support to this thesis. In applying the term "I" to myself, I at once subsume myself under an universal concept: as *an* "I" I am only a member of a whole class. And this is already tantamount to saying that I emerge as a limited and hence as a mortal self.

It can be objected at once that I don't have to have a concept of my own self (as an "I," or whatever) in order to have and to handle all sorts of other concepts; and, if this were true, it would not be the case that I must consider *myself* as a mortal (particular) self in order to rise to the level of conceptual comprehension of the world. But this objection can easily be refuted. Let us consider again the concept of a dog. When I apply it to this particular animal barking in my backyard, I take for granted that the application is done in conformity with the public and publicly recognized rules. I therefore assume that all rational knowers would agree with me in the application of precisely this concept to precisely this animal. And so, in my capacity of *a* rational knower, I consider myself as only one particular member of the whole class (or community) of rational knowers. I thus have a conception of myself as a limited, finite, and hence mortal self—a self that must succumb to the power of death. This important theme returns time and again in Hegel: if man is to rise to the level of Concept, he must destroy and uproot his particularity by facing up to the thought of his death. "[T]he life of mind [*Geist*] is not one that shuns death, and keeps clear of destruction; it endures death and in death maintains its being" (*PhM* 93).

The examples of ordinary class concepts can at best be considered only as stepping stones for approaching the Hegelian *Begriff* as such—the topic of the *Logic of Concept*. In effect, Hegel makes it quite clear (*SL* 602; *Enc.* I, 164) that the ordinary class concepts— the work of understanding (*Verstand*) and not of the truly dialectical reason (*Vernunft*)—represent thinking in its poorest and most mutilated form. They are mechanically abstracted from particulars and then arranged at random in the mind of the knower. They thus lack any systematic interconnectedness, and their abstract universality does not allow us to grasp conceptually the wealth of the concrete reality they must ultimately refer to. They slide over the surface of things while leaving the things' essences forever beyond our grasp. In contrast to such superficial concepts, the genuinely rational *Begriff* is the accomplished unity of thought and being. On the one hand, *Begriff* is a conception, a thought. But, on the other hand, this conception is embodied in the inner essence of the thing conceived: it is "the soul (*Seele*) of the concrete" (*SL* 602).

These themes are familiar to any reader and interpreter of Hegel. Kojève's own contribution is to link up firmly the Hegelian *Begriff* with the finitude of man. As we recall from our earlier discussion of Labor, according to Kojève the unity of thought and being is possible only because the "being" here at issue is a *humanized* being—a man-made world embodying human conceptions. Briefly, we are in a position to grasp the inner nature of things, for we are dealing with things as they have been shaped and fashioned by us in the (historically unfolding) process of Labor. Now, since this process of shaping and fashioning things is guided by a conceptual comprehension, and since man's ascent to the level of such comprehension presupposes his consciousness of himself as a *mortal* creature, it follows that the human activity of world-making—that is, human Time, due to which the Hegelian *Begriff* can be said to exist in the first place[33]—is sustained by man's sense of his finitude.[34] And if the Concept (as the accomplished unity of thought and being) is thus the creation of the mortal agents that we are, one is perfectly warranted in denying the Concept an eternal status and in asserting that "there is" Concept only as long as there are men.[35] Nothing more is needed to make us think of Heidegger's celebrated phrase: *" 'There is' truth only in so far as Dasein is and as long as Dasein is"* (*BT* 269).

Kojève is prepared to take the next—and final—step in drawing this parallel between Hegel and Heidegger. Since the Concept—the unity of thought and being—can be said to exist only in and through the activities of mortal human agents, and since the philosophy of Hegel is the ultimate self-knowledge of the Concept, Hegel's entire philosophizing is sustained by a lucid awareness and acceptance of human mortality (*ILH* 379). Hegel's philosophy is thus radically "atheistic" (*ILH* 527); it is the philosophy of human finitude, essentially identical with the Heideggerian analytic of Dasein (ibid.).

The problematic we are pursuing here—the problematic of time and its finitude—requires that we first establish clearly the sense in which time is to be called finite. In Heidegger, time is finite, for the original temporalizing of Dasein—the source of *any* notion of time—is deployed through human attitudes toward death, the ultimate *limit* of Dasein as a self-interpreting creature. But is the meaning of man's limitation by death the same in Hegel as it is in Heidegger?

This is indeed Kojève's claim, but his own commentary on Hegel allows us to raise serious doubts about the claim's soundness and justification. "If, then, death is a manifestation of the Negativity in Man . . . it is the transformation of his *real being* into *ideal concept* . . . According to Hegel, Man rises 'for the first time' . . . to the *conceptual and discursive* consciousness in general through the risk of life accepted without any necessity'' (*ILH* 523; my italics). Let us now unpack this long passage. If an individual's free risk of life in the struggle for recognition allows him to transform his "real being" into "ideal concept," then the entire struggle for recognition turns out to be a form of dialogue—an interchange of signs and demonstrations, through which both combatants attempt to establish themselves as instances of that very special "ideal concept" that Hegel calls "pure self-consciousness'' (*PhM* 234). Both combatants aim at testing in practice a *conception* each of them has of himself and of his adversary; both of them expose themselves to *the same* kind of danger in order to earn *the same* kind of title. "This risk is always and everywhere—and *with all* (*chez tous*)—the same'' (*LH* 185). My death as envisioned by me and my adversary's death as envisioned by him are thus—both for me and for him—mere instantiations of a common concept. Nothing could be further from the doctrine of Heidegger, where the meaning of my death to me is in principle incommensurable with the meaning of my death to others—to all others (*BT* 283–284). This is why, in Heidegger, my encounter with my death *isolates* me from the others: it spells the collapse of the public discourse and indeed of the public realm as such. In contrast, the Hegelian risk of death during the struggle—the risk through which an individual first asserts himself as capable of accepting his own mortality—is in fact a *mode of communication* between the two combatants, insofar as both of them are jointly acting out and testing their common conception of the purpose, the circumstances, and the participants of the struggle.

We shall arrive at exactly the same conclusion by concentrating on the struggle as it erupts not at the dawn but toward the end of history—in the terror of the French Revolution. Kojève attributes great importance to this experience as described in the *Phenomenology of Mind* (*PhM* 599–610). For, on his interpretation (*ILH* 144, 194, 558) of Hegel's analysis, through the revolutionary terror individuals are reaching out for honor and dignity which were denied to them until then. By unleashing the rule of terror—of the unconditioned violence sweeping away *everybody's* attachment to merely private, particular pursuits and interests—the revolutionized individuals expose themselves freely to the risk of death, and they thus rise to the proud title of *citizens*. But, again, the title is a *shared* one. The reign of terror is seen in the *Phenomenology* as the practical outcome of Rousseau's idea of the *volonté générale:*[36] the revolutionary practice is meant to act out and to confirm the idea of a community of men bound together in universal will. Violence is the great equalizer abolishing all distinctions of classes, ranks, etc., and allowing all individuals to prove themselves as autonomous agents, free of the slavish attachment to life. And so—even if we agree with such an interpretation of Terror—revolutionary violence is only the vehicle of a *conception* that the individuals *share* and that they try to implement in their *common* practice. Their exposure to death is thus—to return to Kojève's terminology—the transformation of their "real being" into "ideal concept."

To sum up, man's consciousness of death is indeed, as Kojève argues, the condition of possibility of the Hegelian Concept. But one must add at once that the Concept ends up by sublating its own condition of possibility, since for Hegel man's consciousness of death is itself part and parcel of the conceptual comprehension of reality. We thus find ourselves at the very antipodes of the Heideggerian analytic of human finitude. Far from uncovering that finitude, we have buried it even deeper than the common sense did, for we can now talk about "transcending" (*ILJ* 526) and "sublimating" (*ILH* 516) death in the universe of discourse and discursively guided practices ("History").

This excursus on death was necessary, for it brings us to the core of our problematic in the present chapter. The finitude of human temporality is due to man's awareness of his ultimate limit in death. To gloss over that limit in some way is thus tantamount to glossing over the finitude of human temporality.

Now, the reason why a *philosophical* theory of time is bound to fail unless it comes to terms with the finitude of human temporality can be put in quite orthodox and traditional terms. As Heidegger keeps insisting (*BT* 377, 457), we cannot account for some important features of time as ordinarily understood unless we consider it as derived from the finite temporality of Dasein. Thus to gloss over the finitude of human temporality forecloses the possibility of comprehending what we all have in mind when we talk about "time" in our everyday lives. Seen from this angle, Heidegger's criticism of Hegel takes on new colors.

Our "everyday way of experiencing time rightly adheres to" a "priority [of] consuming and passing away" (*BT* 483). Time, we all agree, is something in which we encounter beings as they disappear and cease to be. "It's all over," "it's gone"—such phrases, meant to capture the aspect of temporal *flux,* are indispensable (if not indeed central) to our entire vocabulary of time-related terms. But, Heidegger continues, Hegel is unable to *do justice* to this vocabulary. For "[i]f the essence of time is defined as 'intuited becoming,' then it becomes manifest that time is primarily understood in terms of the 'now'" (ibid.) and "then neither arising nor passing away has any priority in time" (ibid.). Hegel "on occasion characterizes time as 'abstraction of consuming'" (ibid.), but "he is consistent enough to grant no such priority to consuming and passing away" (ibid.), for he cannot "provide dialectical grounds for such a priority" (ibid.).

Is the objection well taken? It would be tempting to reply no. After all, we have seen again and again that Hegel did *not* limit himself to the commonsensical notion of time as a sequence of Nows; we have granted his commentators that he *was* familiar with the notion of human temporality. Heidegger's entire objection, therefore, seems to be based on an unacceptable premise. But to dismiss the objection in this way would be to take it at a most superficial level. For the notion of time as a sequence of Nows is only the crudest example of the general model of time as "something that is present-at-hand" (*BT* 485). The picture of time as a sequence of Nows closes off our access to time not because the Nows are Nows but because they are present-at-hand items. Whether such items are entertained in a crude intuition or in a dialectical conception is of no consequence to Heidegger's argument: "every attempt to fit time into any sort of being-concept must necessarily falter. If one tries to master it with the aid of dialectic, that is an escape, as is all dialectic"[37].

Let us spell this out in more detail.

Human consciousness in general is always, for Hegel, "its own notion" (*PhM* 138). The conscious level of life is arrived at when the self succeeds in breaking down its own immediacy (i.e., its blind immersion in feelings, impulses, sensations, etc.) by subjecting itself to self-criticism and self-articulation. No element in the self's *conscious* life can escape that general law. If, then, the self is to be viewed as a temporal project, the temporality at issue must be all shot through with discourse. The merit of Kojève's commentary was to make this point very clear. As we recall, the agent's future first emerges in a conception the agent has of it; the past is always an object of his knowledge, and what counts as the present is determined by his comprehension of the future and of the past. We recall, too, that every temporal dimension is conceptualized in a *different* way. The future is posited as a set of some as yet unfulfilled possibilities of the agent, the past emerges as the springboard for all of his actions, while the present is understood as the product of a project being realized (*ILH* 369).

But the difference between the temporal dimensions is only one aspect of their full relationship in human temporality as a whole. The other aspect is precisely the aspect of arising and passing away. For example, it is the lot of what exists in the present to pass away and to become past. Similarly, what is first envisioned as the as-yet-unrealized future may soon emerge ("arise") in the present. We can say, then, that the aspect of arising and passing away must find its proper place within any notion of human temporality.

Heidegger's objection can now be articulated in its full force. If the three dimensions of human temporality are items disclosed in a *conceptual comprehension,* then we do *not* have any adequate means to account for the aspect of arising and passing away. In effect, a *change* that can be grasped *conceptually* inherits the quality of a *conceptual change,* of a change, that is, where the elapsed (the "passed away") stages are fully integrated into and preserved in all the following (the "arising") stages. For Hegel, a conceptual change is always *cumulative*:[38] to abandon a conception we have been endorsing until now does not mean to reject it altogether but rather to integrate it into a higher and more complex level of conceptual comprehension. This is how conceptual comprehension unfolds itself in both the *Science of Logic* (in the element of pure thinking) and in the *Phenomenology of Mind* (in the experience of a human self). Thus nothing is *irretrievably lost* in the life of spirit;

nothing is gone for good or truly over; everything can be saved by being transformed into an element of the (ever-growing) conceptual whole.

It is not important, then, to Heidegger's overall argument against Hegel, whether time is seen as a sequence of Nows or as the unfolding of spirit in search of self-knowledge. For in this second case, too, time is built up from the present-at-hand items: from representations and conceptions of the self.[39] The true meaning of "arising and passing away" must be covered up by this model of time since, as we recall, all such merely present-at-hand models emerge from the *in*authentic temporality of Dasein, that is, from the temporality of men bent on forgetting the vulnerability and the powerlessness of their condition. In order to face up to arising and passing away of finite beings man would have to face up to *his own* arising and passing away. He prefers instead to gloss over his powerlessness by denying time power over him.[40] But the arising and passing away cannot be glossed over without destroying our entire understanding of time. On this issue Heidegger—with Proust—is firmly against Hegel and, it seems, closer to the nature of things.

The contrast between Heidegger's and Hegel's final words on time can now be fully brought out. Heidegger, we recall, has built his theory of time around the notion of human finitude; and he was then unable to reconstruct the connection between the notion of finite temporality and the notion of time endorsed by men as they search for and find a measure of security in the world. Hegel, it seems, took the opposite path. For Hegel, the temporal unfolding of spirit just *is* the way in which spirit establishes its rule in and over the world. Hence the discovery (in Absolute Knowledge) of the source of time in the activity of spirit does not isolate man from the public realm—as was the case in Heidegger, where Dasein's (anxious) grasp of finite temporality was sufficient to break the bond between the self and the public world—but, on the contrary, strengthens his tie with it. The vulnerability and the powerlessness of man's condition in the world are sublated in the universality of the Concept; and, with our sense of vulnerability and powerlessness glossed over, arising and passing away cannot find their proper articulation.

Our conclusions in this chapter are thus strictly parallel to the conclusions we have arrived at in Chapter 1. The problematic of time imposes *two* requirements which must be met and reconciled. On the one hand—against Heidegger—justice must be done to the claims of a notion of time guiding man's attempts to gain some measure of control over the conditions of his existence. On the other hand—against Hegel—equal justice must be done to a conception of time in which man's powerlessness and vulnerability are faced up to. The message of radical finitude cannot be cast as totally alien to men searching to realize themselves in the world; while, conversely, the temporal vocabulary employed by such men cannot appear entirely meaningless to a man lucidly aware of his own finitude.

VIOLENCE

Conclusion

Let us first envision a collapse of the social order and an outbreak of violence leading to an all-out life-and-death struggle among men.[1] Above anything else, the man I confront in the struggle—the other—is a member of my own species. On account of this basic fact our conflict will exhibit a number of very special, indeed unique, features.

To begin with, given that the other is a member of *my own* species, his powers and capacities are essentially similar to my own, and so his threat to me cannot be neutralized by any determinate means at my disposal. Whatever I can mobilize against him— the weaponry, the intelligence, the will—he is, or may be, capable of mobilizing against me. This statement does not express an ordinary empirical truth. All my actual and possible encounters with the other are perceived from within my foreknowledge of him as a member of my own species. And so, when I probe and identify the weak spots in the other's position, I do it with a sense that he may be capable of matching my strengths with his own. Such a conception of the other is due to the sheer fact of his generic identity with me.

Since *nothing* can be confidently counted on in a life-and-death struggle with the other, my adversary emerges as a threat to all my purposes, including my purpose of staying alive. My vulnerability and exposure are now total. Hence, when I envision the prospect of a life-and-death struggle, I am brought face-to-face with the lack of a firm foundation at the root of my being. And this is another way of saying that the other's threat opens up a *world* for me. I cannot cling to a limited, parochial niche—a tradition, a territory, etc.— for no niche can offer me shelter in a life-and-death struggle. I open up to the world insofar as I realize the unreliability of any local environment to give me a secure protection against the other.

I can thus no longer naively identify with my immediate self. For this self is now within the reach of the unmanageable power of the other. Confronted with this power in a life-and-death struggle, I can depend on nothing to secure the realization of my personal goals and strategies. All of them are now put under a question mark, since the other can block them all in a head-on clash with me. I cannot *take for granted* my personal life, and hence everything I cling to, all my desires, aspirations, and dreams emerge as vulnerable and exposed. I thus gain a perspective broader than the one of my immediate self: I am capable of viewing things with an awareness of the finitude and the limitation of my self.

Threatening my life in an all-out exchange of violence, the other brings me face-to-face with the prospect of my death. Let us add immediately—for this will soon become crucial to our entire argument—that the menace of death imposed upon me by the other exhibits the very same features that it does to a man gripped by the Heideggerian *Angst*. To begin with, the sense of being totally vulnerable to the other's violence is not gained through some form of empirical observation and generalization. In the same stance in which I acknowledge myself to be a human individual living among other individuals I also acknowledge myself as exposed to the possibility of human violence. Since the sense of being thus exposed to a mortal danger is part and parcel of the foreknowledge shaping my relations with others, and since I am a *human* self only to the extent to which I stand in some network of such relations, the sense of my exposure to death belongs to me merely because of my status as a human individual. Furthermore, this existential *certainty* of my death cannot be separated from the *indefiniteness* of death's menace to me: death must be perceived as capable of striking at me anywhere and at any moment. If I could localize the threat of death, if I could enclose it within some limited spatial and temporal parameters, then my life would be free of it at least beyond those parameters; there would thus be a slice of my life where I would not have to define myself as vulnerable. But death can threaten me at any moment and in any place, for the other's threat is in principle beyond my powers. There is nothing I can count on to erase my vulnerability to him. And this is sufficient to explain why the evidence of my mortality is ''not of a graded kind.'' In effect, when I consider the other in his first and simplest determination—his power is similar to mine, for he is generically identical with me, he is of my own kind—I need not and cannot grade and measure the deadly menace that he represents to me. The menace is beyond measuring and beyond grading, for there is *nothing* I can rely upon to bring his power under my control.

It is important to emphasize that the emergence of the other as capable of imposing upon me the sense of my ultimate limit is due only to my perception of him as an (at least potential) adversary in a life-and-*death* struggle. Let us spell this out in more detail. If the other is not perceived as my adversary in a life-and-death struggle, he at once falls under an image I have assigned to him in *my* goals and strategies. He may, of course, put an end to *some* of my goals and strategies. But none of such failures amounts to the imposition of the sense of ultimate limit—of finitude—upon me. I can adapt to all of them either by learning to live with them, or even by reinterpreting them as successes. My vulnerability can be gotten around, for it was not total to begin with. I can always "pick up the pieces" and "get on with my life." Needless to say, I won't be able to do any such thing once the other pulls the trigger of a gun aiming at my temple. No exercise in self-interpretation can get around *that* kind of a limit. And I have no power to silence the voice bringing me the message of total vulnerability, for the messanger is beyond all my means and all my powers.

But—as both Descartes and Heidegger so clearly saw—the message of my total vulnerability and powerlessness is the skeptical message as well. The unmanageable violence the other threatens me with alienates me from all shared practices and vocabularies. The available means of pressure and persuasion all break down and collapse as soon as I confront an adversary bent on annihilating me. There is *nothing* I can deploy against the deadly threat of the other, and so the world *as a whole* breaks down for me. From now on, its truths are all pseudotruths to me, and its certainties are all built on sand. Conversely, there is a truth to skepticism, for the skeptical attitude feeds on a genuine aspect of the human condition: the sense of one's total powerlessness in the face of ultimate violence.

While we have not shown, as yet, that the forms of violence *other than* the human life-and-death struggle cannot be at the root of the skeptical attitude, we are already in a position to show why, in any case, the eruption of the life-and-death struggle among men is fully capable of bringing about the conditions needed to account for the emergence of skepticism. The only thing that is required here is that discussion—even as a possibility—disappear entirely from the field of social intercourse in which the struggle is to take place.

For let us suppose, for the sake of argument, that discussion is not altogether destroyed by the eruption of the life-and-death struggle. Let us suppose that the combatants continue to talk in good faith even while pursuing the path of warfare. Now, as long as there is discussion, there is some form of consensus at the beginning, and there is some possibility of a final agreement. It would be logically inconsistent for me to engage my adversary in a genuine and sincere exchange of arguments while assuming at the same time that he is deaf to arguments to begin with. For me to be willing to carry on a discussion with him, he and I must both forgo violence as the way to settle our dispute. Furthermore, I must be convinced that it is not impossible for our discussion to yield positive results. These two conditions are equally necessary here. If I didn't take for granted that my adversary is prepared to forgo violence, I would not care to begin the discussion, for I would then be committing myself to a true dialogue of the deaf; and if I did not take for granted the possibility—however remote—of reaching an agreement with my adversary, I would not want to waste my time and resources on an exchange that could not prevent the outbreak of violence anyway. As long as I "keep talking" to the other, we are both moving within the realm of discussion, and we are both staying away from violence.

We can see better now why the life-and-death struggle can only take place in the absence of discussion. If I *truly* carry on discussion, then there can *be* no life-and-death struggle. There may still be some exchange of violence, but it will be a limited exchange, employed as a means of pressure upon a partner with whom I will ultimately want to talk. I may try to "make him reasonable" by a threat or a limited use of force, but I am still aiming at bringing him to the discussion table. Violence, here, is not absolute, but relative, and it is relative to a clear purpose I have assigned to it *within* the realm of discussion. This sort of violence is more like a signal to the other, a means of communicating with him. But then there is and there can be no life-and-death struggle in store. There can be no such struggle forthcoming, since a seriously meant and pursued life-and-*death* struggle is, by definition, indifferent to the survival of my adversary and is thus logically incompatible with the intention to engage him at some point in an exchange of arguments. A struggle conducted within the horizon of possible discussion is thus *not* a life-and-death struggle. To be sure, there may be a very thin line between, on the one hand, a limited and partial exchange of violence meant to make the other change his terms in the bargaining process and, on the other hand, the ultimate violence of the life-and-death struggle. It nevertheless remains true that the eruption of the latter adds a *new* quality to human conflicts, since it destroys the realm of discussion as such.

Now—to get back to the main thread of our argument—the *skeptical attitude* cannot emerge as a response to a form of violence that is only a signal or a message to my adversary. As long as I know that he is seriously engaged in communicating with me, I know that he is not aiming at my death. His threat is not a total one, and therefore my vulnerability is not total either. But the sense of such a total vulnerability is indispensable to the emergence of skepticism. As long as I don't have a sense of being totally vulnerable I can always fall back upon *some* of my powers and capacities (both cognitive and practical), and I thus have no reason to entirely suspend my reliance upon them. This is why Descartes's philosophical revolution began with the evil demon hypothesis: since I am *totally* powerless in a confrontation with the evil demon, my doubt must be total too. By the same token, if I know that the other will refrain from annihilating me, I do not feel I am in a position of total vulnerability and hence also of total doubt. To sum up: either the violence that the other unleashes against me is only a signal, an element in the universe of discussion, but then the skeptical attitude will not emerge; or else, like the evil demon's violence in Descartes, the violence of the other does lead to the skeptical attitude, but then the violence at issue is not a signal within a basically discursive framework.

This is why the life-and-death struggle as we interpret it in the present study cannot be understood along the lines of the Hegelian model. I already have had the opportunity to discuss and to criticize this model in detail,[2] but some further remarks are needed for our present purposes. As is well known, Hegel's basic assumption is that the combatants fight for *recognition*. They thus have reasons, which they fully share, for exposing themselves to the trial by violence. Their ability to endure their exposure to death will bear witness to their freedom and independence from all ties to life, and it will thus represent a practical demonstration of their rationality—to themselves *and to each other* (*PhM* 230). But if the struggle is thus a form of communicating, a way of "making a point" with one's adversary, then it cannot be a life-and-*death* struggle. In effect, if I am killed or if I kill my adversary then all communication between us is broken and the desired state of recognition is not realized. Hegel, of course, is fully aware of this trivial truth (*PhM* 233). The combatants, therefore, ought not to be seeking death itself but only the demonstration of their ability to confront and to endure the *risk of death* (*Enc.* III, par. 432) in a combat situation. In this case, however, Hegel is in no position to *account* for the eruption of a genuine life-and-death struggle. For if I know beforehand that both I and my adversary will in the end refrain from killing each other, then the alleged "risk of death" is all sham to begin with. I am certain from the very beginning that my adversary will not put his sword through my heart or pull the trigger of his gun; we are both playing at violence, but we are not playing violently; the fight is all ritualized and perfectly inoffensive, and my death can only result from an unfortunate accident which defeats the main purpose of my adversary.[3]

But even if a life-and-death struggle *could* erupt along the lines defined by the Hegelian model, this sort of struggle would not, in any case, bring us one step closer to the sort of violence capable of generating the skeptical attitude. For if the purpose of the combatants' courage and sacrifice is the demonstration of their autonomy as rational selves—that is, of their common ability to think and act independently of a slavish attachment to life—then their life-and-death struggle cannot mean a breakdown of their shared understanding, and it cannot entail the alienation of an individual from the realm of public practices and vocabularies. Quite the contrary! By entering the struggle I declare my allegiance to a *role* (of a "free and independent self-consciousness"). Both I and my adversary act out such roles while clashing with each other, and both of us take for granted a common understanding of those roles. We must both challenge each other to a fight in order to erect a stage upon which we shall jointly enact the drama of recognition. Consequently, the violence of death with which the other threatens me during the struggle can be fully accommodated by the rational self that I am. The experience of such a violent encounter with the other fills a slot—the most important one, to be sure—in the unfolding structure of my rationality. Or, to put it in the Hegelian parlance, this experience is only a stage through which the rational self is returning to itself. Since, in Hegel, consciousness of death means only—in Kojève's phrase—the transformation of an individual's "real being" into an "ideal concept," the Hegelian model of the life-and-death struggle will not supply the conditions needed to account for the collapse of the conceptual framework as a whole. To supply such an account, we must stop considering the struggle's violence as a display of shared meanings and conceptions, as the combatants' means for establishing themselves in their roles of rational selves. The struggle's violence ought not to be seen as a way of sending a message to one's adversary, as a form of communicating and exchanging signals with him. We must not shrink from talking about *blind violence*. Only *this* kind of violence cannot be mediated and accommodated by a shared conceptual framework. And this is why any such framework must collapse as a whole.

It can now be objected to us that not much progress has been accomplished over the theories of evil demon and anxiety. For, it would seem, the violence of the life-and-death struggle is no way closer to *ordinary* life than the violence those two theories set up as the ultimate limit of human powers. Like the evil demon, like the "indefinite" and "measureless" menace of death, the final showdown of the life-and-death struggle threatens me from *outside* of ordinary life. While giving birth to the sense of total powerlessness and exposure—and hence also to the skeptical alienation from the public discourse—the life-and-death struggle's apocalyptic potential is not encountered by ordinary men engaged in ordinary pursuits, be they practical or cognitive. And so, it seems, the ultimate violence we were searching for in this study is once again shifted onto a purely speculative level.

I would like to suggest that the objection is misconstrued. The life-and-death struggle—the ultimate form of human violence—is not like a thunderbolt striking out of the blue the unsuspecting men of ordinary life. The eruption of a no-holds-barred exchange of violence among men is prepared in the lineaments of their ordinary, daily ways of associating and living together. The life-and-death struggle looms at the horizon of escalating ordinary conflicts, fueled by contradictory interests of groups and individuals, by the clash of values and ideologies, by the rising temperature of passions, and so on. This is what our ordinary language suggests with its own resources: we say (and we are aware) that a conflict can "get out of hand," or that it can "escalate beyond control," etc. Or, again, we are not oblivious to the possibility of some tensions and conflicts leading a community "to the brink of chaos."

Let us try to grasp more clearly the kinds of situations referred to by such and similar expressions. On the one hand, we are dealing here with what begins as ordinary conflicts playing themselves out on the stage of ordinary life. But, in the process of those conflicts growing and gathering momentum, the participants go beyond that initial stage. Having begun as social agents acting within the framework of social practices, they now take one last and final step through which they deny and repudiate their own status as members of a social community. This denial, we can see, is not entirely alien to the ordinary conflicts maturing and developing within the public world. Rather, the denial—the repudiation, by man, of his own status as a communal being, a member of a public realm—emerges as the term of a trend snowballing *within* the public realm. And so the destruction of the public realm—and of my own identity as determined by that realm—is brought about by a development *not entirely discontinuous* with the public realm itself. The life-and-death struggle takes place, and can be expected to take place, when the bond among men begins to slacken and when their conflicts set them further and further apart.

At the same time, the life-and-death struggle is *not entirely continuous* with the ordinary life. The ordinary conflicts must get "out of hand" and "beyond control"; and this pinpoints the element of *novelty* brought about by the emergence of the life-and-death struggle. Its eruption is delineated in the escalating ordinary conflicts, but, when it comes, it goes over and above them, since it destroys the entire arena—the public realm as such—within which they are defined, pursued, and resolved. Or, to put it still differently, the step through which the social man denies his own sociality by plunging into unrestrained violence is not—and it cannot be—simply another mode of social interaction. For a social man, the denial of the social as such spells the emergence of a *new* quality.

Thus life-and-death struggle is both continuous and discontinuous with the ordinary life. It is continuous, for the ordinary life is the soil where the seeds of that ultimate violence are planted and where they grow and develop. It is discontinuous, for the explosion of the life-and-death struggle destroys that very soil—the public realm—which prepared its emergence. The soil *can* be destroyed, for the public realm's existence is not secured by the operation of some natural laws; it is sustained by human commitments and by a fragile consensus built around them. The consensus will not survive if men's commitments to it weaken and disintegrate. It is this fragility and nonnaturalness of human consensus that leaves an opening for violence. A society may thus succeed in removing—due to its technological power—the possibility of natural threats into the realm of farfetched abstractions; but the same society remains exposed to the threat of disintegration of its underlying consensus. Germany's recent history offers a sobering case in point.

The two requirements needed to account for the two main components of the skeptical attitude—(1) skepticism emerges from man's discovery of *total* unreliability of his powers and is thus expressive of man's sense of total powerlessness and vulnerability in the world; (2) skepticism cannot emerge as entirely alien to the practices and epistemic standards of ordinary life, where our vulnerability and powerlessness are only partial—can now be brought together. *Human* violence—and it alone—allows us to build a bridge between these two requirements. As partner in a consensus, the other allows me to have a measure of security and hence a measure of confidence in my powers and capacities; I can thus securely fall back upon and take for granted at least some of my beliefs and certainties. As adversary in a life-and-death struggle, however, the other makes me totally powerless and vulnerable. And these two faces of the other are both continuous (the life-and-death struggle erupts as the term of a trend taking place *within* the public realm) and discontinuous (the life-and-death struggle adds a new quality to conflict, for it means the *denial* of the public realm as such).

These are the two faces of the other: the other is inside and outside the ordinary life; his threat is both conditional and unconditional, both partial and total. It *makes sense* to me to envision the other as stripping me of all my safety nets and exposing me to annihilation. It also *makes sense* to me to envision such a threat as not materializing and the other as malleable to bargain with and control. The possibility of being *totally vulnerable* is delineated in what takes place within the ordinary life; but, at the same time, the sense of *diminishing and diminished vulnerability* cannot be relegated to the status of an escapist notion sustaining the commonsensical man's false feeling of security. The dialogue between the skeptic and the man of common sense—the dialogue that could be established neither in Descartes nor in Heidegger—can now take place. Since the life-and-death struggle's threat is delineated in the partial and determinate conflicts occurring within ordinary life, the man of common sense is not entirely puzzled by the voice of the skeptic. The threat of annihilation represented—however vaguely and remotely—by the other, conveys to the man of ordinary life some sense of the general unreliability of all public practices and vocabularies. As shields against the violence directed at and against him by the other, these practices and vocabularies break down and hence cannot be taken for granted anymore. The man of ordinary life gains a sense of what it is like to suspend his allegiance to the public discourse (to discover that discourse's limitation and unreliability) through the same stance through which he perceives ordinary conflicts as escalating toward an all-out reign of violence. Conversely, the man whose perspective—the skeptical perspective—reflects the sense of his total vulnerability is now capable of vindicating the perspective of common sense. For the one who makes him totally vulnerable—the other—is also a partner in a social consensus, where all conflicts and threats are only partial and conditional and where at least some of man's beliefs and certainties can once again be taken for granted. Or, to put it still differently, the ordinary epistemic attitude is not an illusory escape strategy of a common sense uneducated by philosophy, for the security provided by the *suspension* of the life-and-death struggle supplies the framework within which men can think and act relying confidently upon their native powers and capacities. If doubts emerge, they are always special and entertained for special reasons; their solution calls for special tests conducted in conformity with determinate rules and practices. No doubt is cast upon man's epistemic position as a *whole*.

The problematic of time as we discovered it and discussed it in Chapter 2 has led us to the difficulties strictly parallel to those of Doubt. It was not possible, we found out, to reconcile time's radical finitude with the (much more familiar to us all) features of time perceived by men as they attempt to gain some mastery over the conditions of their lives. Both aspects of time—its radical finitude and its everyday features—were indispensable for any satisfying account of time, and yet, we found, such major philosophical enterprises as those of Hegel and Heidegger failed to carry out the desired conceptual reconciliation. These failures, let us also recall, were due to the one-sided conceptions of human vulnerability. Since, in Heidegger, death is defined as the *absolutely other* of the public realm, there can be no link at all between, on the one hand, the threat of death in all its "certainty" and "indefiniteness" and, on the other hand, whatever it is that man has deployed and secured in his capacity of a builder of the public realm. Death—Heideggerian death—strikes from *outside* of that realm. Consequently, the radical finitude of time can only be conveyed in an apocalyptic message of the philosopher (speaking from the platform of anxiety) which awakens no echo in the mind of the ordinary man. For the philosopher, then, all notions of time spawned by the ordinary man are irrelevant; for the ordinary man, in turn, the philosopher's discourse is totally unintelligible, since it has no continuity whatsoever with the discourses sustaining our everyday existence in the public world. In Hegel, we found, the situation is reversed. Since the continuity between the ordinary and the philosophical discourse about time is bought at the price of glossing over time's finitude, the discourse of the philosopher is merely a more sophisticated way of articulating the conception of time endorsed by men bent on achieving security in life and thought. Heidegger's objections against Hegel, we found, are then perfectly valid and well taken.

The similarity of the problems encountered in our two chapters suggests the similarity in the required solutions. If the notion of the human violence allowed us to bridge the gap between the ordinary and the philosophical conceptions of Doubt, then, we can hope, the same notion may allow us to discover the link between the ordinary and the philosophical notions of Time.

In a life-and-death struggle with the other, my vulnerability and powerlessness are driven to their ultimate limit: I am *totally* exposed and, for that reason, aware of myself as being under the ever real threat of death. Any merely present-at-hand notion of time is thus inadequate to capture the temporality of the life-and-death struggle: I am brought face-to-face with the radical finitude of time. This finite time, we can immediately notice, exhibits the ordering of dimensions (future-past-present) characteristic of human temporality:

1. My adversary in a life-and-death struggle imposes himself upon me as a power capable of bringing about my *end;* I thus first encounter him through a sense of the (finite) *future;* it is due to him that I gain a sense of the permanent possibility of not having any possibilities. Since, as we saw earlier, a genuine life-and-death struggle cannot be a contest aiming at extraction of a mythical ''recognition'' but a clash beyond any conceptual mediation, this *priority of the future* can never be abolished and sublated—as it was in Hegel—in the security of a Presence. And this is why the notion of ''arising and passing away'' can find its proper place

within the temporality of the struggle. For the struggle, when not falsely idealized into a struggle for recognition, not only gives me a sense of my own perishability, but—since this sense has now ceased being glossed over and dissolved (as in Hegel) in a conceptual comprehension—it also allows me to gain a sense of the arising and passing away of persons and things around me.

2. In discovering myself as a finite and limited self I discover my determinateness, that is, my *past*. In effect, if a life-and-death struggle may bring about my end, it must be the case that I *am* a determinate self, defined by specific qualities and relations. What makes up that determinateness of my self is nothing other than what is already fixed and established as my past: my background, my life history, my habits, my dispositions, etc. And so, a sense of the future disclosed to me in a life-and-death struggle opens up a sense of the past.

3. In becoming lucidly aware of myself as limited, I allow the present to stand out and to get through to me. As I can no longer cling to my expectations and anticipations—all of them are now put under a question mark due to the other's threat to me—I cease to consider my surroundings from a goal-oriented, utilitarian perspective; I am open and receptive to the present. This *autonomy* of the present, let us add immediately, is not an isolated, inner state of the self. It can never be absent from actions and attitudes displayed during the life-and-death struggle. In effect, my past can never be taken for granted in a life-and-death confrontation with another man, as there is nothing in that past capable of giving me a secure foothold against him. And so I must put a *distance* between my past and my present; my present must emerge as *new* with respect to the past. I cannot follow passively my inclinations and my habits; I cannot confidently depend upon my background and my achievements; I am forced to improvise and to create, for the other's threat does not allow me the luxury of resting on my laurels—on *any* laurels. To be sure—as was argued in detail elsewhere[4]—I must also acknowledge and utilize my past. For to carry on the struggle *effectively,* I must make the fullest possible use of my powers, capacities, and achievements; I must thus confront the danger from the springboard of the past. Still, in a life-and-death struggle this reliance upon the past can never be complete, as I must always be prepared to break with the established patterns of my life in order to confront the challenge of the other.

Since there is nothing capable of neutralizing the other's mortal threat, and since this threat makes me into a self defined by finite temporality, the finite temporality can have no ground. Wherever I go, I cannot escape the other; whatever I do, I am powerless to prevent him from undoing it; no matter what means and devices I array against him, they are all vulnerable to his power. Hence the temporal striving of my self can find no secure station at which to rest. This is why the possibility of a no-holds-barred struggle among men (and it alone) deploys the openness of the World: the World can be different from some definite, local region, from a mere environment, because the other's threat is not merely local and definite either. The openness of the World is but the objectified counterpart of the open-endedness of the human struggle.

Now, if the emergence of finite temporality is due to the challenge of the other, then its *continuity* with the ordinary notion(s) of time can be accounted for. In effect, the other's threat to me is not—or not entirely—like the threat of Descartes's evil demon or of Heideggerian death. For the other is not only my adversary in a life-and-death struggle; he is also my partner in a peaceful consensus of the public world. *Violence is not altogether alien to peace, while peace is not altogether alien to violence.* The point was made earlier and we shall not repeat it again. If it is valid, though, then the temporality of ordinary life ceases to be irrelevant *even when* considered from the point of view of time's radical finitude; and thus the link between these two conceptions of time—the ordinary and the philosophical—ceases to elude us. The time of ordinary life is founded on a suspension of the life-and-death struggle by the consensus sustaining the public realm. Given this consensus among men, their search for security finds a foundation upon which they are able to take things for granted and to plan for the future without being undermined in those endeavors by death's apocalyptic threat to them at every stage of their lives. But, again, the conception of such a threat is not altogether alien to and discontinuous with man's everyday practices. For the ordinary conflicts dealt with through these fragile practices may, in the end, escalate beyond control and thus destroy the very public realm in which they originated. And then the ordinary, commonsensical temporality will *of itself* yield the place to the temporality of the life-and-death struggle.

Notes

Introduction

1. For a systematic exposition of this view see E. Cassirer, "Drittes Buch, Erstes Kapitel: Descartes," in *Das Erkenntnisproblem in der Philosophie und Wissenschaft der neueren Zeit* (Berlin: B. Cassirer Verlag, 1911).

2. "here we shall treat of things only in relation to our understanding's awareness of them . . . " (HR, I, 41).

3. One point where, in the *Rules*, Descartes's position has not yet fully matured concerns the role of the imagination: its contribution to knowledge is still considered essential in the *Rules,* and this is at odds with the fully developed doctrine of the *Meditations*.

4. The process of this transformation of nature is *labor,* and hence there is a close link between Descartes's conception of active subjectivity and the historicist ontologies that begin with and follow in the footsteps of Hegel. For in the process of changing nature through labor man also comes to change *himself,* and it then becomes possible, and indeed necessary, to work out a new conception of *history* as the process of self-transformation of man. In this process human needs, values, and forms of association become ever more complex and refined so that, in the end, man's dominion over nature will not be considered complete unless man realizes those new, historically emerging, forms of his life.

5. T. Hobbes, *Leviathan* (London: Penguin Books, 1968), p. 150.

6. "*Naturall* Power, is the eminence of the Faculties of Body or Mind: as extraordinary Strength, Forms, Prudence, Arts, Eloquence, Nobility. *Instrumentall* are those Powers, which acquired by these, or by fortune, are

means and instruments to acquire more: as Riches, Reputation, Friends, and the secret working of God, which men call Good Luck'' (ibid.).

7. T. Hobbes, *The Elements of Law, Natural and Politic* (London: Frank Cass and Co., 1969), p. 34.

8. Hobbes, *Leviathan,* p. 161.

9. Ibid., p. 151.

10. Ibid., p. 152.

11. "All these ways of Honouring are naturall; and as well within, as without Common-wealths'' (ibid., p. 154).

12. Ibid., p. 150.

13. Ibid., p. 153.

14. Ibid., p. 151.

15. Hobbes, *The Elements of Law,* p. 169; see, too, T. Hobbes, *De Cive or the Citizen* (New York: Appleton-Century-Crofts, 1949), p. 24.

16. L. Strauss, *The Political Philosophy of Hobbes* (Chicago: University of Chicago Press, 1952), chap. 2.

17. Hobbes is not fully consistent in his terminology. While, in the *Leviathan* (p. 184), the expression he uses to convey his point is "glory," in both *De Cive* (p. 25) and *The Elements of Law* (p. 71) he mentions the "vain glory" (which he now contrasts with well grounded and moderate forms of glory) as the root of human conflict.

18. Let us add, however, that the natural equality of men is also essential in Hobbes's account (*Leviathan,* p. 184; *De Cive,* p. 25). For if some men were naturally inferior they would find their situation hopeless to begin with and would never even attempt to enter the struggle they would be bound to lose. But the violence in the state of nature is "a warre . . . of every man, against every man'' (*Leviathan,* p. 185), not just of some against some.

19. Hobbes, *Leviathan,* pp. 185–185; *The Elements of Law,* p. 71; *De Cive,* pp. 25–26.

20. Hobbes, *Leviathan,* p. 184.

21. "Competition of Riches, Honour, Command, or other power'' (ibid., p. 161).

22. "We must needs acknowledge that it must *necessarily* follow, that those men who are moderate . . . shall be obnoxious to the force of others, that will attempt to subdue them. And from hence shall proceed a *general* diffidence in mankind, and mutual fear one of another'' (Hobbes, *The Elements of Law,* p. 71; my italics).

23. "Moreover, considering that many men's appetites carry them to one and the same end; which end *sometimes* can neither be enjoyed in common, nor divided, it followeth that the stronger must enjoy it alone, and that it be decided by battle who is the stronger'' (ibid.; my italics).

24. Hobbes, *Leviathan,* p. 186.

25. Hobbes, *The Elements of Law,* p. 71; my italics.

26. Through his emphasis upon man's activity of world-making, Hobbes—like Descartes—prepares the ground for modern historicism. See L. Strauss, pp. 106–108; see, too, L. Strauss, *Natural Right and History* (Chicago: University of Chicago Press, 1953), pp. 173–177.

27. In this study I will not be concerned with the position Heidegger adopted in his later writings, after his "turn" (*Kehre*). Throughout this entire book I will be concerned only with the specifically modern idea of human subjectivity, while Heidegger's later thought is all devoted to the purpose of "overcoming" modern subjectivism (and indeed Western metaphysics as such). Heidegger himself came to consider *Being and Time* as bound up with the tradition of modern subjectivism. See, for example, M. Heidegger, *Nietzsche,* vol. 4; *Nihilism* (San Francisco: Harper and Row, 1982), p. 141.

28. See P. Hoffman, *The Human Self and the Life and Death Struggle* (Gainesville/Tampa: University Presses of Florida, 1984).

Chapter 1

1. See, for example, J. L. Austin, *Sense and Sensibilia* (New York: Oxford University Press, 1964), pp. 10–11; M. Merleau-Ponty, *Phenomenology of Perception* (London: Routledge and Kegan Paul, 1962), pp. 374–377.

2. I am restating here G. E. Moore's celebrated argument (see G. E. Moore, *Philosophical Papers* [London: George Allen and Unwin, 1959], p. 151).

3. A. Kenny has argued convincingly that these two hypotheses are equivalent at least in the context of Descartes's sceptical argument (see A. Kenny, *Descartes* [New York: Random House, 1968], pp. 35–36.

4. "I shall then suppose, not that God who is supremely good and a fountain of truth, but some evil genius not less powerful than deceitful, has employed his whole energies in deceiving me; I shall consider that the heavens, the earth, colours, figures, sound and all other external things are nought but the illusions and dreams of which this genius has availed himself in order to lay traps for my credulity; I shall consider myself as having no hands, no eyes, no flesh, no blood, nor any senses, yet falsely believing myself to possess all these things" (HR, I, 148).

5. (HR, I, 60). It is, therefore, a mistake to interpret Descartes's analysis of dream illusions as providing sufficient support for his doubt. For a representative sample of such an interpretation of Descartes see B. Stroud, *The Significance of Philosophical Scepticism* (Oxford: Clarendon Press, 1984), chap. 1.

6. See M. Gueroult, *Descartes selon l'ordre des raisons,* vol. 1 (Paris: Aubier-Montaigne, 1953), pp. 132–137. See, too, E. Cassirer.

7. "Descartes aux Curateurs de l'Université de Leyde" (4 Mai 1647), in *Descartes: Correspondence,* ed. Charles Adam et Gérard Milhaud (Paris: P.U.F., 1936–1963), p. 300.

8. See Charles B. Guignon, *Heidegger and the Problem of Knowledge,* (Indianapolis: Hackett Publishing Company, 1983), p. 174.

9. Ibid., pp. 244–245.

10. B. Pascal, *Pensées* (London: Penguin Books, 1966), pp. 66–72.

11. *"The mood has already disclosed, in every case, Being-in-the-world as a whole, and it makes it possible first of all to direct oneself towards something"* (*BT* 176).

12. Heidegger conveys this important point in several ways. In "On the Essence of Truth" he tells us that he wants to explore "the ground of the inner possibility of the open comportment which *pregives a standard* [my italics], which possibility alone lends to propositional correctness the appearance of fulfilling the essence of truth at all" "On the Essence of Truth," in M. Heidegger, *Basic Writings* Harper and Row, (New York: 1977), p. 125. In *The Essence of Reasons* Heidegger talks about "ontological truth" which, as "transcendental founding," "lies 'at the basis'" of every "ontical truth" (Evanston: Northwestern University Press, 1969), p. 117.

13. *BT* 264–265. Additional clarifications can be found in "On the Essence of Truth," pp. 132–137.

14. In other words, anxiety suspends Dasein's entire understanding of what there is: "in the face of anxiety the utterance of the 'is' falls silent" (M. Heidegger, "What Is Metaphysics," in *Basic Writings,* p. 103).

15. "this *authentic* disclosedness modifies with equal primordiality both the way in which the 'world' is discovered (and this is founded upon disclosedness) and the way in which the Dasein-with of Others is disclosed. The 'world' which is ready-to-hand does not become another one 'in its content,' nor does the circle of Others get exchanged for a new one; but both one's Being towards the ready-to-hand understandingly and concernfully, and one's solicitous Being with Others, are now given a definite character in terms of their ownmost potentiality-for-Being-their-Selves.

"Resoluteness, as authentic Being-one's-Self, does not detach Dasein from its world, nor does it isolate it so that it becomes a free-floating 'I'" (*BT* 344).

16. "One must note that in such formalizations the phenomena get levelled off so much that their real phenomenal content may be lost, especially in the case of such 'simple' relations as those which lurk in significance. The phenomenal content of these 'Relations' and 'Relata' . . . is such that they resist any sort of mathematical functionalization" (*BT* 121–122).

17. Thus Heidegger speaks of "average understanding and of the state-of-mind belonging to it" (*BT* 211).

18. I owe this expression to Hubert L. Dreyfus. I am also indebted to him for many fruitful insights into the function of the Heideggerian *Das Man*. Dreyfus's own interpretation of *Being and Time* stresses the role of the "undifferentiated character of Dasein" (*BT* 69) which, Dreyfus thinks, cuts across both the authentic and the inauthentic mode. It must be noted, however, that the text of *Being and Time* is extremely sparse in the references to this "undifferentiated" mode of Dasein. In addition, it is not at all clear how such a concept could ever be reconciled with the standard Heideggerian views on anxiety or with Heidegger's derivation of the public world from the *in*authentic Dasein's flight from its own mortality. For more detail on Dreyfus's interpretation see Hubert L. Dreyfus, *A Commentary on Division One of "Being and Time"* (Boston: M.I.T. Press, 1986), forthcoming.

19. Kant was well aware of the need to attribute some *reality* to the "I think" of pure apperception, and this is why—Heidegger thinks—he was ultimately led back to the precritical view of the self as an enduring substance (*BT* 367).

20. "The totality-of-significations of intelligibility is *put into words*. To significations, words accrue" (*BT* 204). "The way in which discourse gets expressed is language. Language is a totality of words—a totality in which discourse has a 'worldly' being of its own" (ibid.).

21. "The resoluteness in which Dasein comes back to itself, discloses current factical possibilities of authentic existing and discloses them *in terms of the heritage* which that resoluteness, as thrown, takes over" (*BT* 435). "With the constancy of the they-self Dasein makes present its 'today.' In awaiting the next new thing, it has already forgotten the old one. The 'they' evades choice . . . Lost in the making present of the 'today,' it understands the 'past' in terms of the 'Present.' On the other hand, the temporality of authentic historicality, as the moment of vision of anticipatory repetition, *deprives* the 'today' of its character *as present*, and weans one from the conventionalities of the 'they'" (*BT* 443–444).

22. "The scepticism which ends with the abstraction 'nothing' or 'emptiness' can advance from this not a step farther, but must wait and see whether there is possibly anything new offered, and what that is—in order to cast it into the same abysmal void" (*PhM* 137).

Chapter 2

1. "*die Zeit . . . ist . . . der daseinde Begriff selbst*," in G. W. F. Hegel, *Sämtliche Werke*, vol. 2, *Die Phänomenologie des Geistes* (Leipzig, 1928), p. 38.

2. *vorlaufende Entschlossenheit*.

3. Although the similarity between Kant's and Heidegger's positions on the present issue is attested to by, above all, Heidegger's treatment of Kantian schematism in *Kant and the Problem of Metaphysics*, other places

can be found where this similarity is forcefully brought out by Heidegger. For example, in *The Metaphysical Foundations of Logic* Heidegger does not hesitate to use his own special terminology in explaining how the Kantian categories apply to sensible appearances: ''Kant tries to understand the essence of categories in such a way that categories can be real determinations of objects (of appearances) without having to be empirical properties (of appearances). If determinations of being are not ontic properties of the things that are, in what way do they still belong to *realitas*, to the what-content of objects? Their reality, their belonging to essential content, is a transcendental reality, a finite, *horizonal-ecstatic* [my italics] reality'' (Bloomington: Indiana University Press, 1984), p. 65.

4. *Gegenwärtigen.* Heidegger now stresses (*BPP* 306) that the enpresenting of entities can be done either inauthentically *or* authentically. And this seems to represent a shift of emphasis with respect to the doctrine of *Being and Time* where the related stance of ''making-present'' was attributed almost exclusively to the inauthentic Dasein. But, in spite of a terminological unclarity, there is no contradiction in Heidegger's position. As I discuss this point later on, in connection with the status of horizonal schemata, I will here limit myself to mentioning the essential. Since the authentic Dasein is not an otherworldly self but a participant in the public world, an authentic individual too will produce and surround himself with things—without, however, *losing himself* in that activity.

5. ''On the basis of the *temporality* that grounds the Dasein's transcendence, the Dasein's Temporality makes possible the understanding of being'' (*BPP* 302).

6. ''Der Raum ist die *unmittelbare daseiende* Quantität, der Begriff an ihm selbst als unmittelbar oder in dem Elemente der Gleichgültigkeit und des Auseinanderfallens seiner Momente. Der Unterschied ist aus dem Raume herausgetreten, heisst: er hört auf, diese Gleichgültigkeit zu sein, er ist für sich in seiner ganzen Unruhe, nicht mehr paralysiert . . . Diese reine Quantität als reiner für sich daseiender Unterschied ist . . . *die Zeit*'' (G. W. F. Hegel, *Sämtliche Werke,* vol. 20, *Jenenser Realphilosophie: Die Vorlesungen von 1805–1806,* [Leipzig: F. Meiner, 1932], p. 10).

7. Ibid. p. 6; see, too, *Enc.* II, 29.

8. ''The point, the being-for-self, is consequently rather the *negation* of space, a negation which is posited in space'' (*Enc.* II, 29).

9. *Enc.* II, par. 257, Zusatz. Kant already has made this point. See Kant, *Critique of Pure Reason* (New York: St. Martin's Press, 1965), A411–A412.

10. A. Koyré, ''Hegel á Iena''; reprinted in A. Koyré, *Etudes d' histoire de la pensée philosophique* (Paris: Gallimard, 1971).

11. A. Koyré, ''L' évolution philosophique de Martin Heidegger,'' in *Etudes d'histoire,* p. 280.

12. A Koyré, ''Hegel à Iena,'' p. 184.

13. Ibid., p. 174.

14. Ibid.

15. "As to time . . . The principle of quantity, of difference which is not determined by the notion, and the principle of equality, of abstract, lifeless unity, are incapable of dealing with that sheer restlessness of life and its absolute and inherent process of differentiation" (*PhM* 104).

16. A. Koyré, "Hegel à Iena," pp. 155–157, 165–167.

17. Hegel's idea of "genus" ought not to be confused, of course, with the (abstract) "natural genus" of a zoologist or a botanist. For more detail see H. Marcuse, *Hegels Ontologie und die Grundlegung einer Theorie der Geschichtlichkeit* (Frankfurt: Klostermann, 1932), pp. 268–270.

18. "Die Grenze oder das Moment der Gegenwart, das absolute Dieses der Zeit oder das Jetzt, ist absolut negativ einfach, absolut alle Vielheit aus sich ausschliessend . . . " (G. W. F. Hegel, *Sämtliche Werke,* ed. cit., vol. 18, *Jenenser Logik, Metaphysik und Naturphilosophie,* p. 203).

19. Ibid.

20. A. Koyré, "Hegel à Iena," p. 177.

21. "diese Zukunft ist selbst in der Tat nicht Zukunft, sie ist das die Gegenwart Aufhebende . . . ist sie vielmehr die Gegenwart, die aber ebenso (nach) ihrem Wesen das Nichtsein ihrer selbst oder die Zukunft ist" (Hegel, *Jenenser Logik, Metaphysik und Naturphilosophie,* p. 203).

22. Ibid., p. 204.

23. "Aber das Ehmals ist selbst nicht für sich, es ist ebenso das durch Zukunft zum Gegenteil seiner selbst werdende Jetzt, und es also nicht abgesondert von diesen; es ist an sich selbst nur dieser ganze Kreislauf, die reale Zeit, die durch Jetzt und Zukunft Ehmals wird" (ibid.).

24. Ibid., p. 206.

25. *BT* 418–421. However, let us note a striking change in Heidegger's position after the celebrated *Kehre:* "The attempt in *Being and Time,* section 70, to derive human spatiality from temporality is untenable" (*On Time and Being* [New York: Harper and Row, 1977], p. 23).

26. See P. Hoffman, *The Anatomy of Idealism, Activity and Passivity in Kant, Hegel, and Marx* (The Hague: Martinus Nijhoff, 1982), pp. 72–74.

27. G. W. F. Hegel, *Jenenser Realphilosophie: Philosophie des Geistes,* vol. 19 of *Sämtliche Werke,* p. 229. See, too, *PhM* 232: "The presentation of itself, however, as pure abstraction of self-consciousness consists in showing itself as a pure negation of its objective form or in showing that it is fettered to no determinate existence, that it is not bound at all by the particularity everywhere characteristic of existence as such, and is *not* tied up with life."

28. *Jenenser Realphilosophie: Die Vorlesungen von 1805–1806,* vol. 20, pp. 198–199.

29. *IHL* 374. But see especially Alexandre Kojève, *Kant* (Paris, 1973).

30. A. Kojève, *Kant,* pp. 126–127.

31. "It is as *discursive project* that the future is *really present* as future . . . [T]he present, and hence the past of the project are penetrated and determined by the future, which subsists in it in form of the discourse" (*ILH* 547).

32. "What is called unspeakable is nothing else than what is untrue" (*PhM* 160).

33. We are touching here upon the core of Kojève's treatment of the relationship between Concept, Eternity, and Time. The theme is merely outlined in *Introduction à la lecture de Hegel* (see especially *ILH* 336–366). A systematic development of the problematic can be found in Alexandre Kojève, *Essai d'une histoire raisonnée de la philosophie païenne,* vol. 1, *Introduction* (Paris: Gallimard, 1968).

34. I will quote the passage in its French original for fear of distorting a number of subtle points: "Le Concept est Temps. Temps au sens fort du terme, c'est-à-dire un Temps où il y a un Avenir au sens fort aussi, c'est-à-dire un Avenir qui ne deviendra jamais ni Présent ni Passé. L'Homme est l'existence-empirique du Concept dans le Monde. C'est donc l'existence-empirique dans le Monde d'un Avenir qui ne deviendra jamais présent. Or, cet Avenir, c'est pour l'Homme sa *mort,* ce sien Avenir qui ne deviendra jamais son présent; et la seule realité ou présence réelle de cet Avenir, c'est le *savoir* que l'homme a dans le présent de sa mort future. Donc, si l'Homme est Concept et si le Concept est Temps (c'est-à-dire si l'Homme est un être *essentiellement temporel*),—l'Homme est *essentiellement* mortel; et il n'est Concept, c'est-à-dire Savoir absolu ou Sagesse incarnée, que s'il le sait. Le Logos ne devient chair, ne devient Homme, qu'à condition de vouloir et pouvoir *mourir*" (*ILH* 379).

35. "If, then, the Concept is Time . . . the existence of the Concept—and consequently of the Being revealed by the Concept—is essentially *finite*" (*ILH* 380).

36. "This will is not an empty thought of will, which is constituted by giving a silent assent, or an assent through a representative, a mere symbol of willing; it is concretely embodied universal will, the will of all individuals as such" (*PhM* 600–601).

37. M. Heidegger, *The Metaphysical Foundations of Logic,* p. 204.

38. Eugène Fleischmann, *La science universelle ou la logique de Hegel* (Paris: Plon, 1968), p. 33.

39. This is why in his *Hegel's Concept of Experience* Heidegger will consider the Hegelian self as being simply a more refined case of a self defined, as in Descartes, by a purely *representative* attitude toward reality. Such a definition of the self is laid down, according to Heidegger, already in the *Introduction* to the *Phenomenology of Mind.* Given such a merely "representative" model of consciousness, the differences in Hegel's and

Heidegger's ultimate conclusions follow quite naturally. For Heidegger, the primacy of representation reflects the inauthentic Dasein's drive to make the world safe. The drive is a spurious one: whereas the notion of man's mastery over the conditions of his existence is entirely meaningful for Hegel, it is and must be entirely meaningless for Heidegger. Hence the overcoming of the commonsensical view of "objective" time has a different sense for Hegel than it does for Heidegger. Since Absolute Knowledge amounts to the full *presence* of the Concept to itself, the future ceases to exist for the Sage (*ILH* 380). In contrast, the temporality of authentic Dasein is still defined by the future, since the ever-actual possibility of death cannot be smoothed over by any conceptual comprehension—be it even the (inevitably inauthentic) conceptual comprehension of death itself.

40. "Time, therefore, has no power over Notion (*Bergriff*), nor is the Notion in time or temporal; on the contrary, *it* is the power over time" (*Enc.* II, par. 258).

Conclusion

1. For a more detailed treatment of what follows immediately (pp. 117–19) see P. Hoffman, *The Human Self and the Life and Death Struggle* (Gainesville/Tampa: University Presses of Florida, 1984), chaps. 1 and 2.

2. Ibid., chap. 5.

3. Not unexpectedly, a Prussian general has shown a much better grasp of the life-and-death struggle than the most famous of all the Prussian philosophy professors. Contrasting the positions of Hegel and Clausewitz, Raymond Aron writes: "The duelists want reciprocally to impose their will not in order to gain recognition of the enemy, but to hold him at their mercy and to extract advantages from him. The war pushed to the extreme [of the life-and-death struggle] does not gain a moral dignity because everybody measures up to death: the ascent is born from unleashed passions, from the high stakes involved, from the revolutionary fermentation" (*Penser la guerre, Clausewitz,* vol. 1 [Paris: Gallimard, 1976], pp. 367–368). It is true, of course, that Clausewitz arrived at his theory by analyzing wars among *nations.* But then the struggle of two individual combatants represents, for Clausewitz, a particularly simple and transparent application of his general model (see Carl von Clausewitz, *On War* [Princeton: Princeton University Press, 1976], p. 75).

4. See Hoffman, *The Human Self and the Life and Death Struggle,* pp. 47–49.

Bibliography
of Works
Cited

Aron, R. *Penser la guerre, Clausewitz*, vol. I. Paris: Gallimard, 1976.

Austin, J. L. *Sense and Sensibilia*. New York: Oxford University Press, 1964.

Cassirer, E. *Das Erkenntnisproblem in der Philosophie und Wissenschaft der neueren Zeit*. Berlin: B. Cassirer Verlag.

Clausewitz, C. von *On War*. Princeton: Princeton University Press, 1976.

Descartes, R. "Descartes aux Curateurs de l'Université de Leyde, 4 Mai, 1647." In *Descartes, Correspondence*. Edited by Charles Adam and Gérard Milhaud. Paris: P.U.F., 1936–1963.

———. *The Philosophical Works of Descartes*, 2 vols., ed. Haldane/Ross. Cambridge: Cambridge University Press, 1970.

Dreyfus, H. L. *A Commentary on Division One of "Being and Time,"* Boston: M.I.T. Press, 1986 (forthcoming).

Fleischmann, E. *La science universelle ou la logique de Hegel*. Paris: Plon, 1968.

Gueroult, M. *Descartes selon l'ordre des raisons*. Vol. I. Paris: Aubier-Montaigne, 1953.

Guignon, Charles B. *Heidegger and the Problem of Knowledge*. Indianapolis: Hackett Publishing Company, 1983.

Hegel, G. W. F. *Die Phänomenologie des Geistes*. Vol. 2 of *Sämtliche Werke*. Leipzig: Meiner, 1932.

———. *Jenenser Logik, Metaphysik und Naturphilosphie*. Vol. 18 of *Sämtliche Werke*, ed. cit.

———. *Jenenser Realphilosophie: Philosophie des Geistes*. Vol. 19 of *Sämtliche Werke*, ed. cit.

————. *Jenenser Realphilosophie: Die Vorlesungen von 1805–1806*. Vol. 20 of *Sämtliche Werke*, ed. cit.

————. *The Phenomenology of Mind*. London: George Allen and Unwin; New York: Humanities Press, 1966.

————. *Hegel's Science of Logic*. London: George Allen and Unwin; New York: Humanities Press, 1969.

————. *Hegel's Philosophy of Nature: Part Two of the Encyclopaedia of the Philosophical Sciences*. Oxford: Clarendon Press, 1970.

————. *Hegel's Philosophy of Mind: Part Three of the Encyclopaedia of the Philosophical Sciences*. Oxford: Clarendon Press, 1971.

————. *Hegel's Logic: Part One of the Encyclopaedia of the Philosophical Sciences*. Oxford: Clarendon Press, 1975.

Heidegger, M. *Being and Time*. New York: Harper and Row 1962.

————. *The Essence of Reasons*. Evanston: Northwestern University Press, 1969.

————. *Hegel's Concept of Experience*. New York: Harper and Row, 1970.

————. "On the Essence of Truth." in *Basic Writings*. New York: Harper and Row, 1977.

————. *On Time and Being*. New York: Harper and Row, 1977.

————. "What is Metaphysics." In *Basic Writings*, ed. cit.

————. *The Basic Problems of Phenomenology*. Bloomington: Indiana University Press, 1982.

————. *Nihilism*. Vol. 4 of *Nietzsche*. San Francisco: Harper and Row, 1982.

————. *The Metaphysical Foundations of Logic*. Bloomington: Indiana University Press, 1984.

Hobbes. T. *De Cive or the Citizen*, New York: Appleton-Century-Crofts, 1949.

————. *Leviathan*. London: Penguin Books, 1968.

————. *The Elements of Law, Natural and Politic*. London: Frank Cass & Co., 1969.

Hoffman, P. *The Anatomy of Idealism: Passivity and Activity in Kant, Hegel, and Marx*. The Hague: Martinus Nijhoff, 1982.

————. *The Human Self and the Life and Death Struggle*. Gainesville/Tampa: University Presses of Florida, 1984.

Kant, I. *Critique of Pure Reason*. New York: St. Martin's Press, 1965.

Kenny, A. *Descartes*. New York: Random House, 1968.

Kojève, A. *Essai d'une histoire raisonnée de la philosophie païenne*. Paris: Gallimard, 1968.

————. *Kant*. Paris: Gallimard, 1973.

————. *Introduction à la lecture de Hegel*. Paris: Gallimard, 1979.

Koyré, A. "L'évolution philosophique de Martin Heidegger." In *Etudes d'histoire de la pensée philosophique*. Paris: Gallimard, 1971.

_____. "Hegel à Iena." In *Etudes d'histoire,* ed. cit.

Marcuse, H. *Hegels Ontologie und die Grundlegung einer Theorie der Geschichtlichkeit*. Frankfurt: Klostermann, 1932.

Merleau-Ponty, M. *Phenomenology of Perception*. London: Routledge and Kegan Paul, 1962.

Moore, G. E. *Philosophical Papers*. London: George Allen and Unwin 1959.

Pascal, B. *Pensèes*. London: Penguin Books, 1966.

Strauss, L. *The Political Philosophy of Hobbes*. Chicago: University of Chicago Press, 1952.

_____. *Natural Right and History*. Chicago: University of Chicago Press, 1953.

Stroud, B. *The Significance of Philosophical Scepticism*. Oxford: Clarendon Press, 1984.

Index

Anxiety, 22–29, 123; and doubt, 22–25; and fear, 25–26, 34–38, 62–63, 78–79; negative and positive function of, 38–40; and ordinary moods, 23–24; and temporality, 80–85. *See also* Death
Aristotle, 65, 75
Austin, J. L., 133n.1

Cartesian Circle, and Heidegger, 49
Cassirer, E., 131n.1
Clausewitz, C. von, and Hegel, 139n.3
Communication, 109–10, 120–21
Consensus, 124, 126

Death, 23–29, 34–38; certainty and indefiniteness of, 35–36, 118, 126; and temporality, 82, 67–68. *See also* Hegel; Violence
Descartes, R., ix–xiii, xvii–xviii, 1–21, 63; on dreaming, 3–15; and Heidegger, 22–23, 33–34, 49, 119; on mathematical truths, 13–15; and the ordinary attitude, ix, 19–21; on sensory illusions, 1–3; on total doubt, 14–20. *See also* Evil Demon

Desire: and recognition, 95–98; and temporality, 94–98. *See also* Hegel
Discussion, 119–20
Doubt, xviii, 1–63, 117–29; and consensus, 125–26; special and ordinary, 3, 9, 13; special and ordinary vs. total and general, ix, 14–15, 19–21, 33–34, 38–39, 45, 62–63, 125–26; and time, xviii, 126–27; total and general, xiii, xviii, 9, 15, 17–19, 25, 49; and violence, 119–21. *See also* Anxiety; Descartes; Heidegger
Dreyfus, H. L., 135n.18

Evil Demon, xiii, 10, 15–21, 63, 123

Fear. *See* Anxiety
Finitude, and death, 35; and inauthenticity, 54–55; and the life-and-death struggle, 117; of temporality in Hegel as interpreted by Kojève, 65–66, 106–10; of temporality in Heidegger, 40, 78, 85, 112–14; of the temporality of the life-and-death struggle, 127–29

Hegel, G. W. F., ix, xviii, 85–114,